ILLUSTRATED LYRICS

EDITED BY ALAN ALDRIDGE

THE

BEATLES

ILLUSTRATED LYRICS

Black Dog & Leventhal

Paperbacks

First published in Great Britain in 1969 and 1971 by Macdonald Unit 75.
Reissued in 1990 by Macdonald & Co. (Publishers) Ltd, London & Sydney.
This edition published by arrangement with Houghton Mifflin Company Inc.
This Black Dog & Leventhal paperback edition published in 2006.

Published by
Black Dog & Leventhal Publishers
151 West 19th Street
New York, NY 10011
Manufactured in China

ISBN-10: 1-57912-616-2
ISBN-13: 978-1-57912-616-2

h g f e d c b a

Dedicated to

who didn't see it and to
Rita, Miles and Saffron who did.

I'd love to turn you on

Illustration from article 'Beatles Sinister Songbook' – The Observer November 1967

Foreword

How many superlatives have been used to describe the Beatles?

There is no doubting their impact on popular music in the 1960s, when this book was first published in two volumes. But their influence is still prevalent. Their recordings, original compositions and even their movies have had a dramatic effect on the routes taken by the entertainment industry and will probably continue to do so – even though the surviving members of the group have long gone their separate ways and will never again create new material together.

Alan Aldridge's introduction to the first volume captures the essence of the Beatles' appeal then and now, and his aim to present a book which is as entertaining to the eye and the imagination as a Beatles album is to the ear still holds true today.

Dreams of the reunification of the Fab Four were finally shattered with the assassination of John Lennon in front of his home in December 1980. This book, which contains contributions by some of the greatest artists of our time, is thus inevitably more of a retrospective tribute than a celebration of a decade's style. The magic remains, and A Splendid Time is Guaranteed for All.

Introduction

It is almost irreverent and certainly irrelevant to think of the Beatles in mundane terms as the pop group who became the biggest rock and roll attraction ever. While their early appearances caused unprecedented scenes of mass hysteria, their music has developed into a fascinating social history of our generation and its culture. It was the realisation of the elevation of pop music and allied pop culture by the Beatles which drew my interest to the possibility of producing this book.

I first became aware of the depth of the lyrics to the Beatles' songs when I went to a party in 1967 during the Sergeant Pepper era. Someone whispered in my ear that *Lucy in the Sky with Diamonds* was a song about an LSD trip. Although ambiguity in the lyrics to popular music was no new thing, the scale of the various interpretations of the songs on the Sergeant Pepper album so intrigued me that I began reading *all* the lyrics of Beatles' songs and finding, or imagining, all kinds of hidden meanings. One phrase in particular staggered me: "keeping her face in a jar by the door", from *Eleanor Rigby*. This seemed to me pure surrealism. And as this was an area in which I was working in illustrations, I decided in my complete naivety that I should interview the author of the line, Paul McCartney. The result was an article, which when published with my own illustrations, created a deluge of fan mail. It led me directly to begin planning this book of the best Beatles' lyrics.

Altogether, something like 180 songs by the Beatles have been published, but since many of the earlier compositions are very repetitive in theme and would not have provided enough difference in illustration, we were able to weed them out. Having done this we sent lists to the 43 contributors and asked them to tick off the ones they wanted to do. Ironically enough it quickly got to the stage where nearly all the ones *I* wanted to do had been chosen by someone else—but never mind!

What I have tried to do is to present a book which is as entertaining to the eye and the imagination as a Beatles album is to the ear. For an artist it is a challenging exercise to take a lyric and illustrate it. And of course, there is a very long tradition of this. Artists have always illustrated passages from the Bible or from poems, and we have tried to do the same thing here. In a sense, the Beatles are a religion: they turn people on by what they say and by what they represent.

For me, the music and lyrics of the Beatles are a tremendous springboard into the imagination. No matter how good or how bad their poetry may be, it is universal in appeal and that being so, is that much more viable a thing to illustrate.

The lyrics are the catalyst for the artists' imaginations. Some of the illustrations here are very imaginative: others seem straightforward. But maybe that is because I have not caught their meanings first time. I am always staggered for example, at the number of people who listen to *Hey Jude* without understanding it. But I must admit that although I have read all the lyrics very carefully many times, I cannot honestly claim to understand them fully yet. I should like to believe that this book is more than merely a selection of drawings of Beatles' songs. I see it as an illustration of the sixties.

For the section on fan art we advertised widely. Treasured drawings were sent to us in masses. They ranged from 6′ 6″ canvases right down to little pencilled drawings of John and Yoko. We also received large numbers of abusive letters . . . something which was new to me. I suppose when there is a lot of loving directed at something or someone, then there must be a lot of hating too.

The Beatles and their music have captured the tempo of the world today. I believe that the illustrations in this book may illuminate their contribution to the style of their generation.

Alan Aldridge, 1969

'There's a lot random in our songs . . .
writing, thinking,
letting others think of bits—
then bang, you have the jigsaw puzzle'–Paul

Mother Nature's son

Born a poor young country boy –
Mother Nature's son.
All day long I'm sitting singing songs
for everyone.
Sit beside a mountain stream – see
her waters rise.
Listen to the pretty sound of music as
she flies.
Find me in my field of grass – Mother
Nature's son.
Swaying daisies sing a lazy song
beneath the sun.
Mother Nature's son.

**"I've never really done anything to
create what has happened. It creates
itself. I'm here because it happened.
But I didn't do anything to make it
happen apart from saying 'Yes'."–
Ringo**

Good day sunshine

Good day sunshine, good day sunshine,
good day sunshine.
I need to laugh, and when the sun is out,
I've got something I can laugh about.
I feel good in a special way,
I'm in love, and it's a sunny day.
Good day sunshine, good day sunshine,
good day sunshine.
We take a walk, the sun is shining down,
burns my feet as they touch the ground.
Good day sunshine, good day sunshine,
good day sunshine.
And then we lie beneath a shady tree,
I love her and she's loving me.
She feels good, she knows she's looking
fine,
I'm so proud to know that she is mine.
Good day sunshine, good day sunshine,
good day sunshine.
Good day sunshine, good day sunshine.

**"Don't forget to say I was wearing a
very big smile"—Linda Eastman to
reporters after her marriage to Paul**

All I've got to do

Whenever I want you around, yeh,
All I gotta do
Is call you on the phone and you'll come
running home,
Yeh, that's all I gotta do.
And when I wanna kiss you, yeh,
All I gotta do
Is whisper in your ear the words you
want to hear,
And I'll be kissing you.
And the same goes for me whenever you
want me at all,
I'll be here, yes I will, whenever you call,
You just gotta call on me, yeh, you just
gotta call on me.
And when I wanna kiss you, yeh,
All I gotta do
Is call you on the phone and you'll come
running home,
Yeh, that's all I gotta do.
And the same goes for me whenever you
want me at all,
I'll be here, yes I will, whenever you call,
You just gotta call on me, yeh, you just
gotta call on me.

Ob-la-di, Ob-la-da

Desmond has a barrow in the market
place.
Molly is a singer in a band.
Desmond says to Molly – girl I like your
face
And Molly says this as she takes him by
the hand.
Obladi oblada life goes on bra
Lala how the life goes on
Obladi oblada life goes on bra
Lala how the life goes on.
Desmond takes a trolley to the jewellers
stores,
Buys a twenty carat golden ring.
Takes it back to Molly waiting at the door
And as he gives it to her she begins to
Sing.
In a couple of years they have built
A home sweet home
With a couple of kids running in the yard
Of Desmond and Molly Jones.
Happy ever after in the market place
Desmond lets the children lend a hand.
Molly stays at home and does her pretty
face
And in the evening she still sings it with
the band.
Happy ever after in the market place
Molly lets the children lend a hand.
Desmond stays at home and does his
pretty face
And in the evening she's a singer with the
Band.
And if you want some fun – take Obladi
Oblada.

Michelle

Michelle ma belle
These are words that go together well, my
Michelle,
Michelle ma belle,
Sont les mots qui vont tres bien ensemble
tres bien ensemble.
I love you, I love you, I love you,
That's all I want to say,
Until I find a way,
I will say the only words I know that
you'll understand.
Michelle ma belle,
Sont les mots qui vont tres bien ensemble
tres bien ensemble.
I need to, I need to, I need to,
I need to make you see,
oh what you mean to me,
Until I do I'm hoping you will know what
I mean.
I love you.
I want you, I want you, I want you,
I think you know by now,
I'll get to you somehow,
Until I do I'm telling you so you'll
understand.
Michelle ma belle,
Sont les mots qui vont tres bien ensemble
tres bien ensemble.
I will say the only words I know that
you'll understand,
my Michelle.

"While we were in India they were all making their plans and I was going to produce Yoko and I would've been producing her had we not fallen in love anyway. But it didn't turn out like that. And now we're together. Yes, it turned out much better, and it's getting better all the time . . ."
—John

Getting better

It's getting better all the time
I used to get mad at my school
the teachers who taught me weren't cool
Holding me down, turning me round
filling me up with your rules.
I've got to admit it's getting better
It's a little better all the time
I have to admit it's getting better
it's getting better since you've been mine.
Me used to be angry young man
me hiding me head in the sand
You gave me the word
I finally heard
I'm doing the best that I can.
I admit it's getting better
It's a little better all the time yes
I admit it's getting better
it's getting better since you've been mine.
I used to be cruel to my woman
I beat her and kept her apart from the things that she loved
Man I was mean but I'm changing my scene
and I'm doing the best that I can.
I admit it's getting better
a little better all the time
Yes I admit it's getting better
it's getting better since you've been mine.
Getting so much better all the time.

Helter skelter

When I get to the bottom I go back to the top of the slide.
Where I stop and I turn and I go for a ride
Till I get to the bottom and I see you again.
Do you, don't you want me to love you.
I'm coming down fast but I'm miles above you.
Tell me tell me tell me come on tell me the answer.
You may be a lover but you ain't no dancer.
Helter skelter helter skelter
Helter skelter.
Will you, won't you want me to make you.
I'm coming down fast but don't let me break you.
Tell me tell me tell me the answer.
You may be a lover but you ain't no dancer.
Look out helter skelter helter skelter
Helter skelter
Look out, cause here she comes.
When I get to the bottom I go back to the top of the slide
And I stop and I turn and I go for a ride
And I get to the bottom and I see you again.
Well do you, don't you want me to make you
I'm coming down fast but don't let me break you.
Tell me tell me tell me the answer.
You may be a lover but you ain't no dancer.
Look out helter skelter helter skelter
Helter skelter
Look out helter skelter
She's coming down fast
Yes she is
Yes she is.

I'm so tired.

I'm so tired, I haven't slept a wink,
I'm so tired, my mind is on the blink.
I wonder should I get up and fix myself a
drink.
No, no, no.
I'm so tired I don't know what to do.
I'm so tired my mind is set on you.
I wonder should I call you but I know
what you'd do.
You'd say I'm putting you on.
But it's no joke, it's doing me harm.
You know I can't sleep, I can't stop my
brain
You know it's three weeks, I'm going
insane.
You know I'd give you everything I've got
for a little peace of mind.
I'm so tired, I'm feeling so upset
Although I'm so tired I'll have another
cigarette
And curse Sir Walter Raleigh.
He was such a stupid git.

**"Touring was murder. We hardly
saw any of America because we had
to stay inside hotel rooms all the
time. And we were always dead
beat"—Ringo**

The word

Say the word and you'll be free,
Say the word and be like me,
Say the word I'm thinking of,
Have you heard the word is love.
It's so fine, it's sunshine,
It's the word love.
In the beginning I misunderstood,
But now I've got it the word is good.
Say the word and you'll be free,
Say the word and be like me,
Say the word I'm thinking of,
Have you heard the word is love.
It's so fine, it's sunshine,
It's the word love.
Everywhere I go I hear it said,
In the good and the bad books that I have
read.
Say the word and you'll be free,
Say the word and be like me
Say the word I'm thinking of
Have you heard the word is love.
It's so fine, it's sunshine,
It's the word love.
Now that I know what I feel must be
right,
I mean to show ev'rybody the light,
Give the word a chance to say,
That the word is just the way,
It's the word I'm thinking of,
And the only word is love.
It's so fine it's sunshine,
It's the word love.
Say the word love,
Say the word love,
Say the word love,
Say the word love.

Drive my car

Asked a girl what she wanted to be,
she said, baby can't you see?
I wanna be famous, a star of the screen,
but you can do something in between.
Baby, you can drive my car, yes I'm
gonna be a star,
baby, you can drive my car, and maybe
I'll love you.
I told that girl that my prospects were
good,
she said, baby it's understood,
working for peanuts is all very fine,
but I can show you a better time.
Baby, you can drive my car, yes I'm
gonna be a star,
baby, you can drive my car, and maybe
I'll love you
Beep beep mm, beep beep yeh!
Baby, you can drive my car, yes I'm
gonna be a star,
baby, you can drive my car, and maybe
I'll love you.
I told that girl I could start right away,
and she said, listen, Babe, I've got
something to say,
got no car, and it's breaking my heart,
but I've found a driver, that's a start.
Baby, you can drive my car, yes I'm
gonna be a star,
baby, you can drive my car, and maybe
I'll love you.
Beep beep mm, beep beep yeh!

The word "John and I would like to do songs with just one note like 'Long Tall Sally'. We get near it in 'The word'. The word is love." – Paul

Drive my car "The truth is, I'm not a car addict. I feel embarrassed having to go into a garage and then pointing vaguely at the car and saying er, I think it's the er, you know, er, that's gone wrong . . ." – Paul

24

When I'm sixty-four

When I get older losing my hair,
many years from now.
Will you still be sending me a Valentine
birthday greetings bottle of wine.

If I'd been out till quarter to three
would you lock the door.
Will you still need me, will you still feed
me,
when I'm sixty-four.
You'll be older too,

25

and if you say the word,
I could stay with you.
I could be handy, mending a fuse
when your lights have gone.
You can knit a sweater by the fireside
Sunday morning go for a ride,

doing the garden, digging the weeds,
who could ask for more.
Will you still need me, will you still feed me,
when I'm sixty-four.
Every summer we can rent a cottage,

in the Isle of Wight, if it's not too dear
we shall scrimp and save
grandchildren on your knee
Vera Chuck & Dave
send me a postcard, drop me a line,
stating point of view

indicate precisely what you mean to say
yours sincerely, wasting away
give me your answer, fill in a form
mine for evermore.
Will you still need me, will you still feed me.
When I'm sixty-four.

A day in the life

I read the news today oh boy
about a lucky man who made the grade
and though the news was rather sad
well I just had to laugh
I saw the photograph
He blew his mind out in a car
he didn't notice that the lights had
changed
a crowd of people stood and stared
they'd seen his face before
nobody was really sure
if he was from the House of Lords.
I saw a film today oh boy
the English Army had just won the war
a crowd of people turned away
but I just had to look
having read the book.
I'd love to turn you on
Woke up, got out of bed,
dragged a comb across my head
found my way downstairs and drank a
cup,
and looking up I noticed I was late.
Found my coat and grabbed my hat
made the bus in seconds flat
found my way upstairs and had a smoke,
and somebody spoke and I went into a
dream
I heard the news today oh boy
four thousand holes in Blackburn,
Lancashire
and though the holes were rather small
they had to count them all
now they know how many holes it takes
to fill the Albert Hall.
I'd love to turn you on.

"I was writing the song with the Daily Mail propped up in front of me on the piano, I had it open at their News in Brief, or Far and Near, whatever they call it. There was a paragraph about 4,000 holes in Blackburn, Lancashire, being discovered and there was still one word missing in that verse when we came to record. I knew the line had to go 'Now they know how many holes it takes to fill the Albert Hall.' It was a nonsense verse really, but for some reason I couldn't think of the verb. What did the holes do to the Albert Hall? It was Terry (Doran) who said 'fill' the Albert Hall."—John

Happiness is a warm gun

She's not a girl who misses much.
Do do do do do do do do
She's well acquainted with the touch of
the velvet hand
Like a lizard on a window pane.
The man in the crowd with the
multicoloured mirrors
On his hobnail boots
Lying with his eyes while his hands are
busy
Working overtime
A soap impression of his wife which he ate
And donated to the National Trust.
I need a fix 'cause I'm going down.
Down to the bits that I left uptown.
I need a fix 'cause I'm going down.
Mother Superior jump the gun
Mother Superior jump the gun
Mother Superior jump the gun
Mother Superior jump the gun
Happiness is a warm gun
Happiness is a warm gun
When I hold you in my arms
And I feel my finger on your trigger
I know no one can do me no harm
because happiness is a warm gun.
Yes it is.

**"I think this is my favourite on The
Beatles album."** – Paul

In my life

There are places I'll remember
all my life, though some have changed,
some forever, not for better,
some have gone and some remain.
All these places had their moments,
with lovers and friends I still can recall,
some are dead and some are living,
in my life I've loved them all.
But of all these friends and lovers,
there is no one compared with you,
and these mem'ries lose their meaning
when I think of love as something new.
Though I know I'll never lose affection
for people and things that went before,
I know I'll often stop and think about
them,
in my life I'll love you more.
Though I know I'll never lose affection
for people and things that went before,
I know I'll often stop and think about
them
in my life I'll love you more.
In my life I'll love you more.

**"There is one thing I used to regret
and feel guilty about. When Ringo
joined us I used to act all big time with
him because I'd been in the business a
bit longer and felt superior. I was a
know-all. I'd been in the sixth form
and thought I'd read a bit, you know.
I began putting him off me, and me
off me."** – Paul

Peter Le Vasseur 1969

The continuing story of Bungalow Bill

Hey, Bungalow Bill
what did you kill
Bungalow Bill?
He went out tiger hunting with his
elehant and gun.
In case of accidents he always took his
mom.
He's the tall American bullet-headed
saxon mother's son.
All the children sing
Hey, Bungalow Bill
What did you kill
Bungalow Bill?
Deep in the jungle where the mighty tiger
lies
Bill and his elephants were taken by
surprise.
So Captain Marvel zapped in right between
the eyes.
All the children sing
Hey, Bungalow Bill
What did you kill
Bungalow Bill?
The children asked him if to kill was not a
sin.
Not when he looked so fierce, his mother
butted in.
If looks could kill it would have been us
instead of him.
All the children sing
Hey, Bungalow Bill
What did you kill
Bungalow Bill?

**"Lots of people who complained about
us receiving the MBE received
theirs for heroism in the war—for
killing people. We received
ours for entertaining other people. I'd
say we deserve ours more.
Wouldn't you?"—John**

Martha my dear

Martha my dear though I spend my days
in conversation
Please
Remember me   Martha my love
Don't forget me Martha my dear
Hold your head up you silly girl look what
you've done
When you find yourself in the thick of it
Help yourself to a bit of what is all
around you
Silly Girl.
Take a good look around you
Take a good look you're bound to see
That you and me were meant to be for
each other
Silly girl.
Hold your hand out you silly girl see what
you've done
When you find yourself in the thick of it
Help yourself to a bit of what is all around
you
Silly girl.
Martha my dear you have always been
my inspiration
Please
Be good to me   Martha my love
Don't forget me Martha my dear.

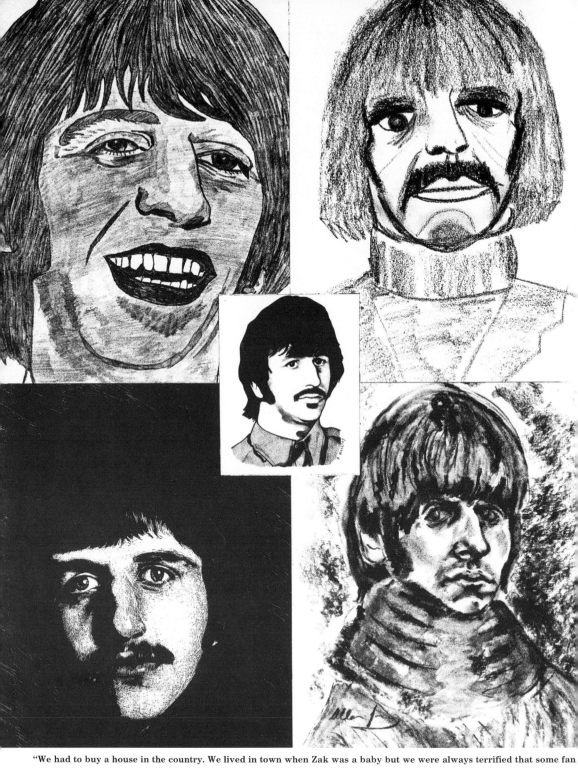

"We had to buy a house in the country. We lived in town when Zak was a baby but we were always terrified that some fan

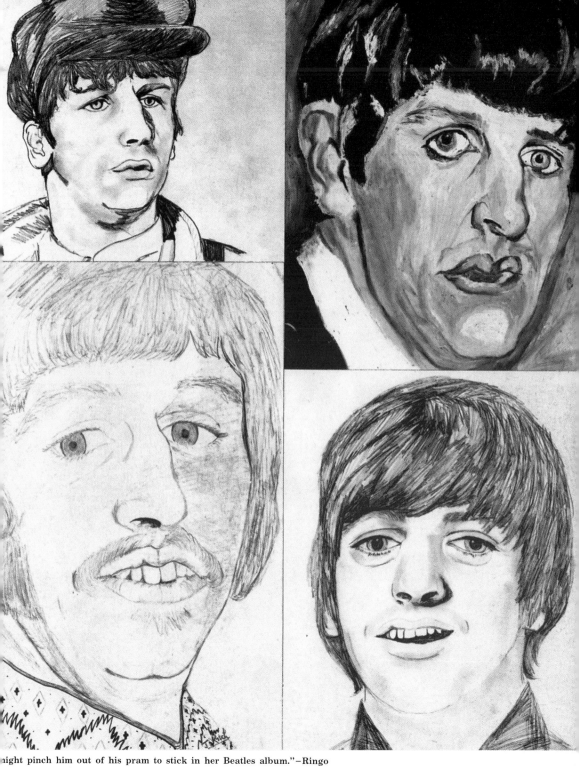

night pinch him out of his pram to stick in her Beatles album."—Ringo

What goes on

What goes on in your heart,
what goes on in your mind?
You are tearing me apart,
when you treat me so unkind,
what goes on in your mind?
The other day I saw you,
as I walked along the road,
but when I saw him with you
I could feel my future fold.
It's so easy for a girl like you to lie,
tell me why?
What goes on in your heart
what goes on in your mind?
You are tearing me apart,
when you treat me so unkind,
what goes on in your mind?
I met you in the morning,
waiting for the tides of time,
but now the tide is turning,
I can see that I was blind.
It's so easy for a girl like you to lie,
tell me why?
What goes on in your heart.
I used to think of no-one else,
but you were just the same,
you didn't even think of me as someone
with a name,
did you mean to break my heart and
watch me die,
tell me why?
What goes on in your heart,
what goes on in your mind?
You are tearing me apart,
when you treat me so unkind,
what goes on in your mind?

**"I used to wish that I could write
songs like the others—and I've tried,
but I just can't. I can get the words all
right, but whenever I think of a tune
and sing it to the others they always
say 'Yeah, it sounds like such-a-
thing,' and when they point it out I see
what they mean. But I did get a part
credit as a composer on one—it was
called What Goes On."—Ringo (his
first self-composition was Don't
Pass Me By on The Beatles album—
1968)**

Misery

The world is treating me bad, misery.
I'm the kind of guy who never used to cry,
The world is treating me bad, misery.
I've lost her now for sure,
I won't see her no more,
It's gonna be a drag, misery.
I'll remember all the little things we've
done,
Can't she see she'll be the only one,
lonely one,
Send her back to me 'cos ev'ry one can
see,
Without her I will be in misery.
I'll remember all the little things we've
done,
She'll remember and she'll be the only
one, lonely one,
Send her back to me 'cos ev'ry one can
see,
Without her I will be in misery.
Oo in misery. Oo in misery.

"Do you remember when everyone began analysing Beatle songs—I don't think I ever understood what some of them

were supposed to be about." – Ringo

Strawberry Fields forever

Let me take you down,
'cos I'm going to Strawberry Fields.
Nothing is real
and nothing to get hungabout.
Strawberry Fields forever.
Living is easy with eyes closed
Misunderstanding all you see.
It's getting hard to be someone.
But it all works out,
it doesn't matter much to me.
Let me take you down,
'cos I'm going to Strawberry Fields.
Nothing is real
and nothing to get hungabout.
Strawberry Fields forever.
No one I think is in my tree,
I mean it must be high or low.

That is you can't you know tune in.
But it's all right.
That is I think it's not too bad.
Let me take you down,
'cos I'm going to Strawberry Fields.
Nothing is real
and nothing to get hungabout.
Strawberry Fields forever.
Always, no sometimes, think it's me,
but you know I know when it's a dream.
I think I know I mean a 'Yes'.
But it's all wrong.
That is I think I disagree.
Let me take you down,
'cos I'm going to Strawberry Fields.
Nothing is real
and nothing to get hungabout.
Strawberry Fields forever.
Strawberry Fields forever.

39

"Everybody thinks Paul wrote it, but John wrote it for me. He's got a lot of soul has John, you know."—Ringo

Good night

Now it's time to say good night
Good night sleep tight.
Now the sun turns out his light
Good night sleep tight.
Dream sweet dreams for me
Dream sweet dreams for you.
Close your eyes and I'll close mine
Good night sleep tight.
Now the moon begins to shine
Good night sleep tight.
Dream sweet dreams for me
Dream sweet dreams for you.
Close your eyes and I'll close mine
Good night sleep tight.
Now the sun turns out his light
Good night sleep tight.
Dream sweet dreams for me.
Dream sweet dreams for you.
Good night good night everybody
Everybody everywhere.
Good night.

MERSE BEAT

Vol. 1 No. 13   **JANUARY 4-18, 1962**

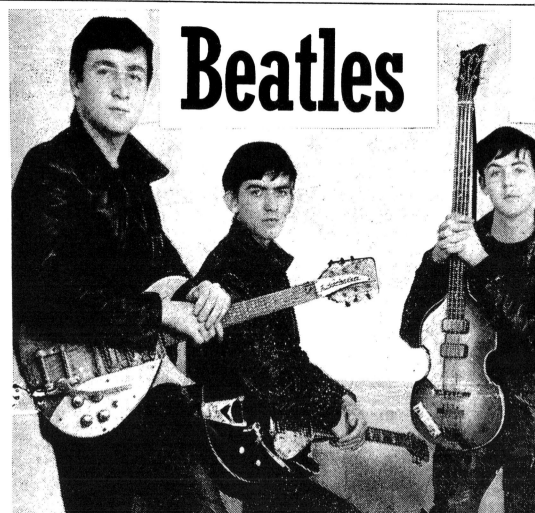

Beatles

JOHN LENNON   GEORGE HARRISON   PAUL McARTNE

NMENTS PAPER

Price THREEPENCE

Top Poll!

FULL RESULTS INSIDE

Cover photograph by Albert Marrion

PETE BEST

"These boys won't make it. Four-groups are out. Go back to Liverpool Mr. Epstein—you have a good business there"—a major executive of a major British record company 1962

43

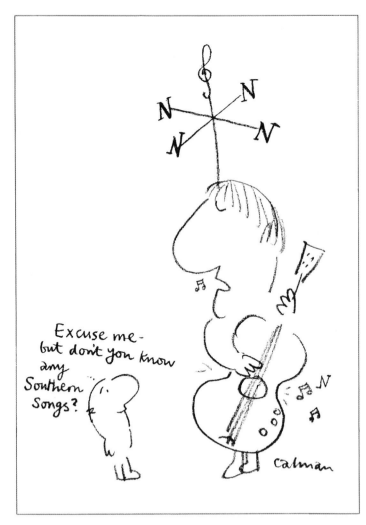

Excuse me – but don't you know any Southern Songs?

calman

"There's no way to pour £4,000,000 into India and make it right" – Paul

Only a Northern Song

If you're listening to this song
You may think the chords are going wrong
But they're not;
He just wrote it like that.
It doesn't really matter what chords I play
What words I say or time of day it is
As it's only a Northern song
It doesn't really matter what clothes I wear
Or how I fare or if my hair is brown
When it's only a Northern song.
When you're listening late at night
You may think the band are not quite right
But they are, they just play it like that
It doesn't really matter what chords I play
What words I say or time of day it is
As it's only a Northern song.
It doesn't really matter what clothes I wear
Or how I fare or if my hair is brown
When it's only a Northern song.
If you think the harmony
Is a little dark and out of key
You're correct, there's nobody there.
It doesn't really matter what chords I play
What words I say or time of day it is
And I told you there's no one there.

Blackbird

Blackbird singing in the dead of night
Take these broken wings and learn to fly.
All your life
You were only waiting for this moment to arise.
Blackbird singing in the dead of night
Take these sunken eyes and learn to see.
All your life
You were only waiting for this moment to be free.
Blackbird fly, Blackbird fly
Into the light of the dark black night.
Blackbird fly, Blackbird fly
Into the light of the dark black night.
Blackbird singing in the dead of night
Take these broken wings and learn to fly.
All your life
You were only waiting for this moment to arise
You were only waiting for this moment to arise
You were only waiting for this moment to arise.

I will

Who knows how long I've loved you.
You know I love you still.
Will I wait a lonely lifetime
If you want me to—I will.
For if I ever saw you
I didn't catch your name.
But it never really mattered
I will always feel the same.
Love you forever and forever.
Love you with all my heart.
Love you whenever we're together.
Love you when we're apart.
And when at last I find you
Your song will fill the air.
Sing it loud so I can hear you.
Make it easy to be near you
For the things you do endear you to me
You know I will.
I will.

I will "I realised that I had been
aware of her for some time. We've
been talking for a long time about
getting married. Then last week
instead of talking about it we
decided to do it. Linda made it
sooner rather than later."—Paul

Here there and everywhere

To lead a better life, I need my love to be
here.
Here, making each day of the year,
changing my life with a wave of her hand.
Nobody can deny that there's something
there.
There, running my hands through her
hair,
both of us thinking how good it can be.
Someone is speaking but she doesn't
know he's there.
I want her ev'rywhere, and if she's beside
me I know I need never care,
but to love her is to meet her ev'rywhere,
knowing that love is to share,
each one believing that love never dies,
watching her eyes and hoping I'm always
there.
I want her ev'rywhere, and if she's beside
me I know I need never care,
but to love her is to meet her ev'rywhere,
knowing that love is to share,
each one believing that love never dies,
watching her eyes and hoping I'm always
there.
To be there and ev'rywhere,
here, there and ev'rywhere.

47

Back in the U.S.S.R.

Flew in from Miami Beach BOAC.
Didn't get to bed last night.
On the way the paper bag was on my
knee.
Man I had a dreadful flight.
I'm back in the U.S.S.R.
You don't know how lucky you are boy
Back in the U.S.S.R.
Been away so long I hardly knew the
place.
Gee it's good to be back home.
Leave it till tomorrow to unpack my case.
Honey disconnect the phone.
I'm back in the U.S.S.R.
You don't know how lucky you are boy
Back in the U.S. Back in the U.S. Back in
the U.S.S.R.
Well the Ukraine girls really knock me
out.
They leave the West behind.
And Moscow girls make me sing and
shout
That Georgia's always on my mind.
I'm back in the U.S.S.R.
You don't know how lucky you are boys
Back in the U.S.S.R.
Show me round your snow peaked
mountains way down south
Take me to your daddy's farm
Let me hear your balalaikas ringing out
Come and keep your comrade warm.
I'm back in the U.S.S.R.
You don't know how lucky you are boys
Back in the U.S.S.R.

Hey Jude

Hey Jude don't make it bad,
take a sad song and make it better,
remember, to let her into your heart,
then you can start to make it better.
Hey Jude don't be afraid,
you were made to go out and get her,
the minute you let her under your skin,
then you begin to make it better.
And anytime you feel the pain,
Hey Jude refrain,
don't carry the world upon your
shoulders.
For well you know that it's a fool,
who plays it cool,
by making his world a little colder.
Hey Jude don't let me down,
you have found her now go and get her,
remember (Hey Jude) to let her into your
heart,
then you can start to make it better.
So let it out and let it in
Hey Jude begin,
you're waiting for someone to perform
with.
And don't you know that it's just you.
Hey Jude, you'll do,
the movement you need is on your
shoulder.
Hey Jude, don't make it bad,
take a sad song and make it better,
remember to let her under your skin,
then you'll begin to make it better.

Hey Jude "It was going to be 'Hey Jules', but it changed. I was driving down to Weybridge one day to see Cynthia (Lennon) and Julian and I just started singing 'Hey Jules, don't make it bad' and then I changed it to 'Hey Jude'. You know, the way you do."–Paul
Back in the U.S.S.R. "When we first started, our idols were Elvis and Chuck Berry. Now they're Marks and Spencers."–Paul

Got to get you into my life

I was alone, I took a ride,
I didn't know what I would find there.
Another road where maybe I
could see another kind of mind there.
Ooh then I suddenly see you,
ooh did I tell you I need you
ev'ry single day of my life?
You didn't run, you didn't lie,
you knew I wanted just to hold you,
and had you gone, you knew in time

we'd meet again for I had told you.
Ooh you were meant to be near me,
ooh and I want you to hear me,
say we'll be together ev'ry day.
Got to get you into my life.
What can I do, what can I be?
When I'm with you I want to stay there.
If I'm true I'll never leave,
and if I do I know the way there.
Ooh then I suddenly see you,
ooh did I tell you I need you,

ev'ry single day of my life?
Got to get you into my life.
Got to get you into my life.
I was alone, I took a ride,
I didn't know what I would find there.
Another road where maybe I
could see another kind of mind there,
ooh then I suddenly see you,
ooh did I tell you I need you
ev'ry single day of my life?
What are you doing to my life?

"We were influenced by our Tamla Motown bit on this. You see we're influenced by whatever's going."—John

Good morning, good morning

Nothing to do to save his life call his wife
in nothing to say but what a day how's
your boy been
nothing to do it's up to you
I've got nothing to say but it's O.K.
Good morning, good morning,
good morning . . .
Going to work don't want to go feeling
low down
heading for home you start to roam then
you're in town
everybody knows there's nothing doing
everything is closed it's like a ruin
everyone you see is half asleep.
And you're on your own you're in the
street.
Good morning, good morning . . .
After a while you start to smile now you
feel cool.
Then you decide to take a walk by the old
school.
Nothing had changed it's still the same
I've got nothing to say but it's O.K.
Good morning, good morning,
good morning . . .
People running round it's five o'clock.
Everywhere in town it's getting dark.
Everyone you see is full of life.
It's time for tea and meet the wife.
Somebody needs to know the time, glad
that I'm here.
Watching the skirts you start to flirt now
you're in gear.
Go to a show you hope she goes.
I've got nothing to say but it's O.K.
Good morning, good morning,
good morning . . .

**"I often sit at the piano, working at
songs, with the telly on low in the
background. If I'm a bit low and not
getting much done then the words on
the telly come through. That's when
I heard Good Morning, Good
Morning . . . it was a Corn Flakes
advertisement."—John**

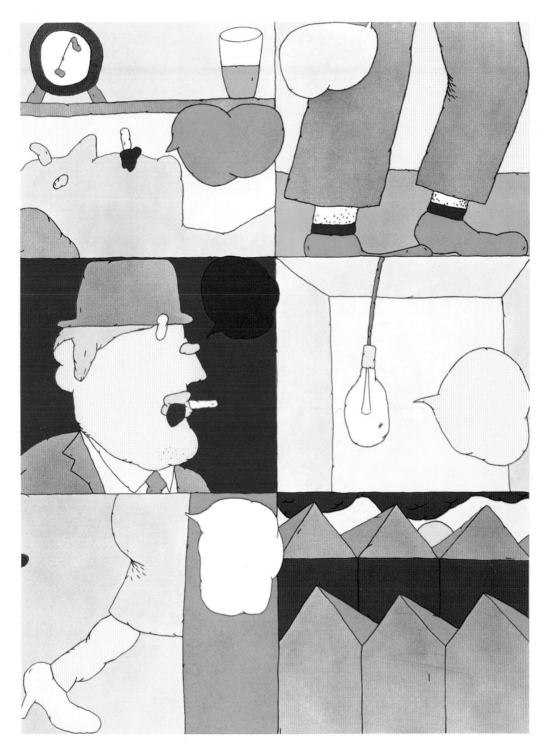

Being For the Benefit of Mr Kite "John has this old poster that says right at the top, 'Pablo Fanques Fair presents the Hendersons For the Benefit of Mr Kite' and it has all the bits that sound strange: 'The Hendersons'—you couldn't make that up."—Paul

Lady Madonna

Lady Madonna children at your feet
wonder how you manage to make ends
meet.
Who finds the money when you pay the
rent?
Did you think that money was heaven
sent?
Friday night arrives without a suitcase
Sunday morning creep in like a nun
Monday's child has learned to tie his
bootlace.
See how they'll run.
Lady Madonna baby at your breast
wonder how you manage to feed the rest.
See how they'll run.
Lady Madonna lying on the bed
listen to the music playing in your head.
Tuesday afternoon is never ending
Wedn'sday morning papers didn't come
Thursday night your stockings needed
mending.
See how they'll run.
Lady Madonna children at your feet
wonder how you manage to make ends
meet.

Being for the benefit of Mr. Kite!

For the benefit of Mr. Kite
there will be a show tonight on
trampoline.
The Hendersons will all be there
late of Pablo Fanques Fair—what a scene.
Over men and horses hoops and garters
lastly through a hogshead of real fire!
In this way Mr. K. will challenge the
world!
The celebrated Mr. K.
performs his feat on Saturday at
Bishopsgate
the Hendersons will dance and sing
as Mr. Kite flies through the ring don't be
late
Messrs. K. and H. assure the public
their production will be second to none
and of course Henry The Horse dances the
waltz!
The band begins at ten to six
when Mr. K. performs his tricks without
a sound
and Mr. H. will demonstrate
ten somersaults he'll undertake on solid
ground.
Having been some days in preparation
a splendid time is guaranteed for all
and tonight Mr. Kite is topping the bill.

Lady Madonna "It sounds like Elvis doesn't it? No—no it doesn't sound like Elvis. It is Elvis—even those bits where he goes very high."—Ringo

"We always got screams up in Scotland, right from the beginning. I suppose they haven't got much else to do up there."—John

Genius of
the Regency
by William Gaunt

ctors' Bosh
by Paul Jennings

Nowhere man

He's a real Nowhere Man,
sitting in his Nowhere Land,
making all his Nowhere plans for nobody.
Doesn't have a point of view,
knows not where he's going to,
isn't he a bit like you and me?
Nowhere Man please listen,
you don't know what you're missing,
Nowhere Man, the world is at your
command.
He's as blind as he can be,
just sees what he wants to see,
Nowhere Man can you see me at all?
Nowhere Man don't worry,
take your time, don't hurry,
leave it all till somebody else,
lends you a hand.
Doesn't have a point of view,
knows not where he's going to,
isn't he a bit like you and me?
Nowhere Man please listen,
you don't know what you're missing,
Nowhere Man, the world is at your
command.
He's a real Nowhere Man,
sitting in his Nowhere Land,
making all his Nowhere plans for nobody.
Making all his Nowhere plans for nobody.
Making all his Nowhere plans for nobody.

"I was just sitting, trying to think of a song, and I thought of myself sitting there, doing nothing and getting nowhere. Once I'd thought of that, it was easy. It all came out. No, I remember now, I'd actually stopped trying to think of something. Nothing would come. I was cheesed off and went for a lie down, having given up. Then I thought of myself as Nowhere Man—sitting in his nowhere land"—John

"At Woolton village fete I met him. I was a fat schoolboy and, as he leaned an arm on my shoulder, I realised that he was drunk. We were twelve then, but, in spite of his sideboards, we went on to become teenage pals."—Paul, in the introduction to John's first book 'John Lennon In His Own Write, 1964'

We can work it out

Try to see it my way,
do I have to keep on talking till I can't go
on?
While you see it your way,
run the risk of knowing that our love may
soon be gone.
We can work it out. We can work it out.
Think of what you're saying,
you can get it wrong and still you think
that it's alright,
think of what I'm saying,
we can work it out and get it straight, or
say good-night.
We can work it out. We can work it out.
Life is very short, and there's no time,
for fussing and fighting, my friend,
I have always thought that it's a crime,
so I will ask you once again.
Try to see it my way,
only time will tell if I am right or I am
wrong,
while you see it your way,
there's a chance that we may fall apart
before too long.
Life is very short, and there's no time,
for fussing and fighting, my friend,
I have always thought that it's a crime,
so I will ask you once again.
Try to see it my way,
only time will tell if I am right or I am
wrong,
while you see it your way,
there's a chance that we may fall apart
before too long.
We can work it out. We can work it out.

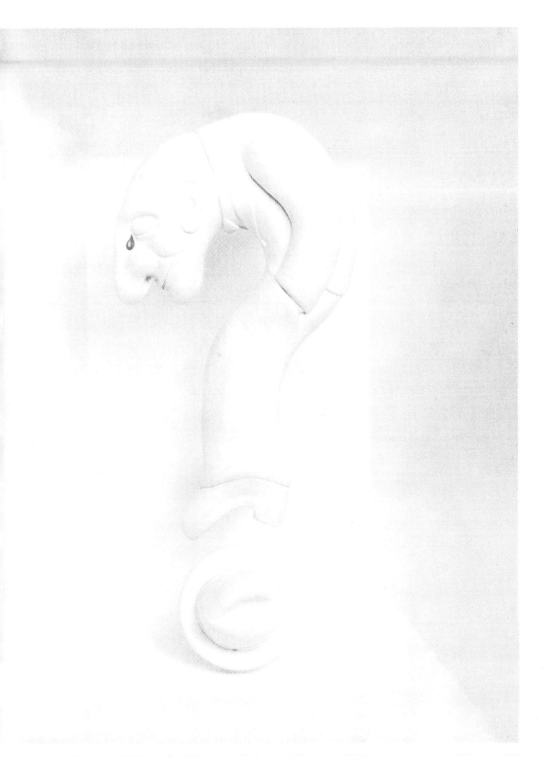

She loves you

She loves you yeh, yeh, yeh,
She loves you yeh, yeh, yeh.
You think you've lost your love,
Well I saw her yesterday—yi—yay,
It's you she's thinking of,
And she told me what to say—yi—yay.
She says she loves you,
And you know that can't be bad,
Yes, she loves you,
And you know you should be glad.
She said you hurt her so,
She almost lost her mind,
And now she says she knows,
You're not the hurting kind.
She says she loves you,
And you know that can't be bad,
Yes, she loves you,
And you know you should be glad.
She loves you yeh, yeh, yeh,
She loves you yeh, yeh, yeh,
And with a love like that,
You know you should be glad.
You know it's up to you,
I think it's only fair,
Pride can hurt you too,
Apologise to her.
Because she loves you,
And you know that can't be bad,
Yes, she loves you,
And you know you should be glad.
She loves you yeh, yeh, yeh,
She loves you yeh, yeh, yeh.
With a love like that,
You know you should be glad.
With a love like that,
You know you should be glad.
With a love like that,
You know you should be glad.
Yeh, yeh, yeh,
Yeh, yeh, yeh.

**"I feel that I'm getting younger.
Even physically. It is partly the diet
because, you see, you are what you
eat. And it is also the fact that I
have met John."—Yoko**

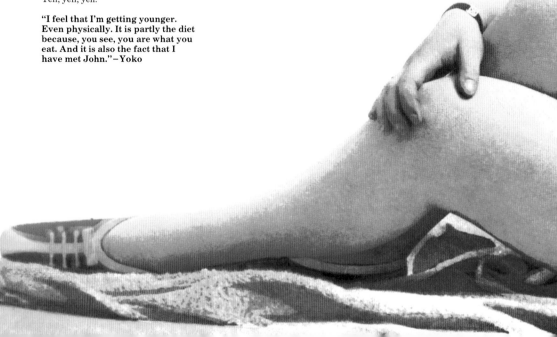

Cry baby cry

Cry baby cry.
Make your mother sigh.
She's old enough to know better.
The king of Marigold was in the kitchen
Cooking breakfast for the queen.
The queen was in the parlour
Playing piano for the children of the king.
Cry baby cry.
Make your mother sigh.
She's old enough to know better.
So cry baby cry.
The king was in the garden
Picking flowers for a friend who came to
play.
The queen was in the playroom
Painting pictures for the children's
holiday.
Cry baby cry.
Make your mother sigh.
She's old enough to know better.
So cry baby cry.
The duchess of Kirkcaldy always smiling
And arriving late for tea.
The duke was having problems
With a message at the local bird and bee.
Cry baby cry.
Make your mother sigh.
She's old enough to know better.
So cry baby cry.
At twelve o'clock a meeting round the
table
For a seance in the dark.
With voices out of nowhere
Put on specially by the children for a lark.
Cry baby cry.
Make your mother sigh.
She's old enough to know better.
So cry baby cry cry cry baby.
Make your mother sigh.
She's old enough to know better.
Cry baby cry
cry cry cry
Make you mother sigh.
She's old enough to know better.
So cry baby cry.

**"It's all over now. It's the end, in a
way, isn't it?" – Diane Robbins,
aged 15, of London on the day Paul
was married**

Ticket to ride

I think I'm gonna be sad,
I think it's today yeh,
The girl that's driving me mad,
Is going away.
She's got a ticket to ride,
She's got a ticket to ri – hi – hide,
She's got a ticket to ride,
But she don't care.
She said that living with me,
Is bringing her down yeh,
For she would never be free,
When I was around,
She's got a ticket to ride
She's got a ticket to ri – hi – hide.
She's got a ticket to ride,
But she don't care.
I don't know why she's riding so high,
She ought to think twice,
She ought to do right by me,
Before she gets to saying goodbye,
She ought to think twice,
She ought to do right by me.

I think I'm gonna be sad,
I think it's today yeh,
The girl that's driving me mad,
Is going away.
She's got a ticket to ride,
She's got a ticket to ri – hi – hide,
She's got a ticket to ride,
But she don't care.
I don't know why she's riding so high,
She ought to think twice,
She ought to do right by me.
Before she gets to saying goodbye,
She ought to think twice,
She ought to do right by me.
She said that living with me,
Is bringing her down yeh,
For she would never be free,
When I was around,
She's got a ticket to ride,
She's got a ticket to ri – hi – hide,
She's got a ticket to ride,
But she don't care.
My baby don't care,
my baby don't care.

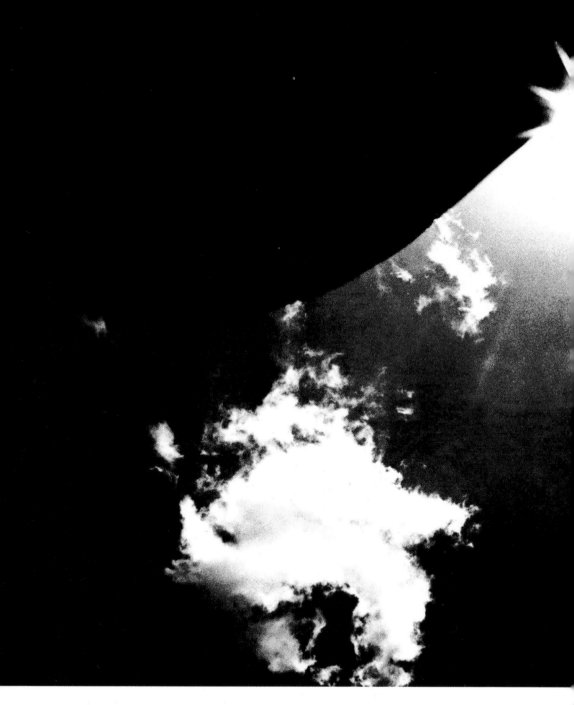

Lucy in the sky with diamonds "This one is amazing. People came up and said cunningly 'Right, I get it, LSD' and it was w[...] at school and brought it home, and he has a schoolmate called Lucy, and John said 'What's that?' and he said 'Lucy in the [...]

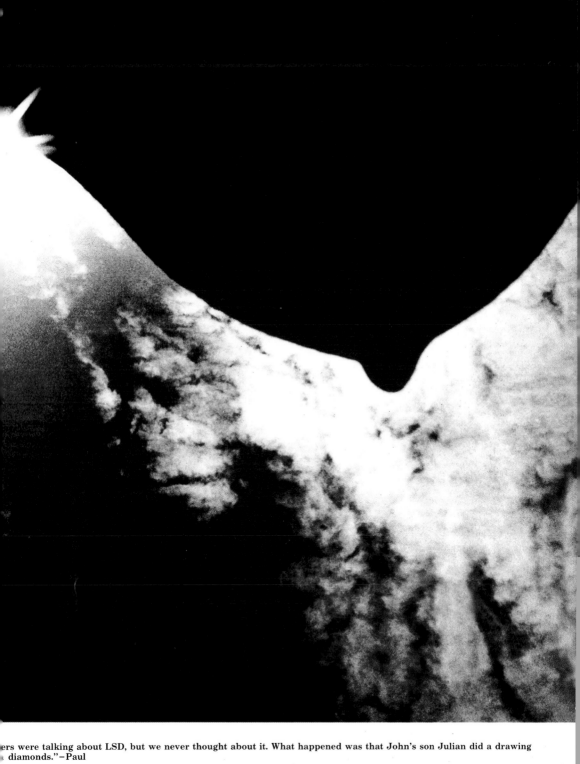

ers were talking about LSD, but we never thought about it. What happened was that John's son Julian did a drawing
diamonds."—Paul

Why don't we do it in the road?

Why don't we do it in the road?
No one will be watching us.
Why don't we do it in the road?

Taxman

Let me tell you how it will be,
There's one for you, nineteen for me,
'Cos I'm the Taxman,
Yeah, I'm the Taxman.
Should five per cent appear too small,
Be thankful I don't take it all,
'Cos I'm the Taxman,
Yeah, I'm the Taxman.
If you drive a car, I'll tax the street,
If you try to sit, I'll tax your seat,
If you get too cold, I'll tax the heat,
If you take a walk, I'll tax your feet.
Taxman.
'Cos I'm the Taxman,
Yeah, I'm the Taxman.
Don't ask me what I want it for
(Taxman Mister Wilson)
If you don't want to pay some more
(Taxman Mister Heath),
'Cos I'm the Taxman,
Yeah, I'm the Taxman.
Now my advice for those who die,
Declare the pennies on your eyes,
'Cos I'm the Taxman,
Yeah, I'm the Taxman.
And you're working for no-one but me,
Taxman.

Lucy in the sky with diamonds

Picture yourself in a boat on a river,
with tangerine trees and marmalade skies
Somebody calls you, you answer quite
slowly,
a girl with kaleidoscope eyes.
Cellophane flowers of yellow and green,
towering over your head.
Look for the girl with the sun in her eyes,
and she's gone.
Lucy in the sky with diamonds,
Follow her down to a bridge by a fountain
where rocking horse people eat
marshmallow pies,
everyone smiles as you drift past the
flowers,
that grow so incredibly high.
Newspaper taxis appear on the shore,
waiting to take you away.
Climb in the back with your head in the
clouds,
and you're gone.
Lucy in the sky with diamonds,
Picture yourself on a train in a station,
with plasticine porters with looking glass
ties,
suddenly someone is there at the
turnstile,
the girl with kaleidoscope eyes.
Lucy in the sky with diamonds.

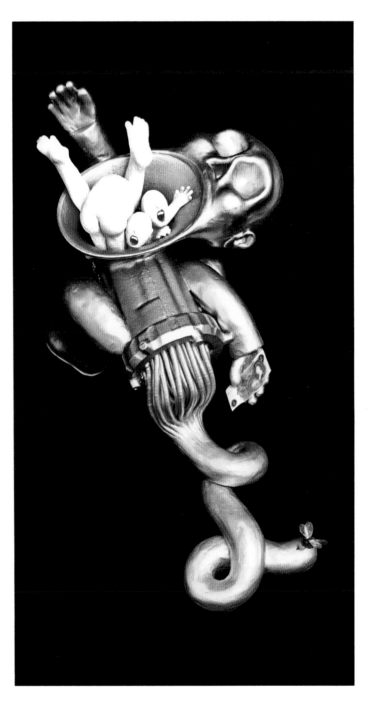

Taxman "I'm down to my last £50,000" – John

Magical Mystery Tour

Roll up–Roll up for the Mystery Tour.
Roll up, roll up for the Mystery Tour.
(roll up) and that's an invitation
Roll up for the Mystery Tour
(roll up) to make a reservation
Roll up for the Mystery Tour
the Magical Mystery Tour is waiting to
take you away
waiting to take you away.
Roll up, roll up for the Mystery Tour
Roll up, roll up for the Mystery Tour
(roll up) we've got ev'rything you need
(roll up) for the Mystery Tour
(roll up) satisfaction guaranteed
Roll up for the Mystery Tour
the Magical Mystery Tour is hoping to
take you away
hoping to take you away now
The Magical Mystery Tour
roll up, roll up for the Mystery Tour.
(roll up) and that's an invitation
Roll up for the Mystery Tour
(roll up) to make a reservation
Roll up for the Mystery Tour
the Magical Mystery Tour is coming to
take you away
coming to take you away
The Magical Mystery Tour is dying to take
you away
dying to take you away–take you today.

**"I suppose if you look at it from the
point of view of good Boxing Day
entertainment, we goofed really. My
dad brought the bad news in to me
this morning like the figure of doom.
Perhaps the newspapers are right–
perhaps we're right." –Paul, after
almost universal criticism of their
Magical Mystery Tour television film.**

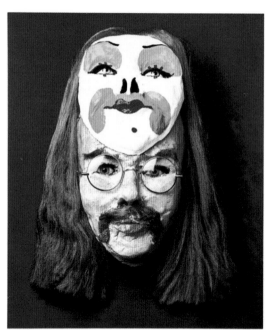

I'm a loser

I'm a loser, I'm a loser,
And I'm not what I appear to be.
Of all the love I have won or have lost,
There is one love I should never have
crossed.
She was a girl in a million my friend,
I should have known she would win in
the end.
I'm a loser, and I lost someone who's
near to me,
I'm a loser, and I'm not what I appear to
be.
Although I laugh and act like a clown,
Beneath this mask, I am wearing a frown,
My tears are falling like rain from the
sky,
Is it for her or myself that I cry.
I'm a loser, and I lost someone who's near
to me.
I'm a loser, and I'm not what I appear to
be.
What have I done to deserve such a fate,
I realise I have left it too late.
And so it's true pride comes before a fall,
I'm telling you so that you won't lose all.
I'm a loser, and I lost someone who's near
to me,
I'm a loser and I'm not what I appear to
be.

Fixing a hole

I'm fixing a hole where the rain gets in
and stops my mind from wandering
where it will go.
I'm filling the cracks that ran through the
door
and kept my mind from wandering
where it will go.
And it really doesn't matter if I'm wrong
I'm right
where I belong I'm right
where I belong.
See the people standing there who
disagree and never win
and wonder why they don't get into my
door.
I'm painting the room in a colourful
way
and when my mind is wandering there I
will go.
And it really doesn't matter if
I'm wrong I'm right
where I belong I'm right
where I belong.
Silly people run around they worry me
and never ask me why they don't get past
my door.
I'm taking the time for a number of
things
that weren't important yesterday
and I still go.
I'm fixing a hole where the rain gets in
and stops my mind from wandering
where it will go.

Rocky Raccoon

Now somewhere in the black mountain
hills of Dakota
There lived a young boy named Rocky
Raccoon.
And one day his woman ran off with
another guy.
Hit young Rocky in the eye Rocky didn't
like that.
He said I'm gonna get that boy.
So one day he walked into town
Booked himself a room in the local saloon.
Rocky Raccoon checked into his room
Only to find Gideon's Bible.
Rocky had come equipped with a gun
To shoot off the legs of his rival.
His rival it seems had broken his dreams
by stealing the girl of his fancy.
Her name was Magill and she called
herself Lill
But everyone knew her as Nancy.
Now she and her man who called
himself Dan
Were in the next room at the hoe down.
Rocky burst in and and grinning a grin
He said Danny boy this is a showdown
But Daniel was hot—he drew first and
shot
And Rocky collapsed in the corner.
Now the doctor came in stinking of gin
And he proceeded to lie on the table.
He said Rocky you met your match.
And Rocky said, Doc it's only a scratch
And I'll be better, I'll be better doc as
soon as I am able.
Now Rocky Raccoon he fell back in his
room
Only to find Gideon's Bible.
Gideon checked out and he left it no
doubt
To help with good Rocky's revival.

Norwegian wood

I once had a girl,
or I should say
she once had me.
She showed me her room,
isn't it good?
Norwegian wood.
She asked me to stay and she told me to
sit anywhere,
so I looked around and I
noticed there
wasn't a chair.
I sat on a rug
biding my time,
drinking her wine.
We talked until two,
and then she said,
"It's time for bed".
She told me she worked in the morning
and started to laugh,
I told her I didn't, and crawled off to
sleep in the bath.
And when I awoke
I was alone,
this bird had flown,
so I lit a fire,
isn't it good?
Norwegian wood.

Help

Help! I need somebody,
help! Not just anybody,
help! You know I need someone,
help!
When I was younger, so much younger
than today,
I never needed anybody's help in any
way,
but now these days are gone I'm not so
self assured,
now I find I've changed my mind I've
opened up the doors.
Help me if you can, I'm feeling down,
and I do appreciate you being round,
help me get my feet back on the ground,
won't you please please help me?
And now my life has changed in oh so
many ways,
my independence seems to vanish in the
haze,
but ev'ry now and then I feel so insecure,
I know that I just need you like I've
never done before.
Help me if you can, I'm feeling down,
and I do appreciate you being round,
help me get my feet back on the ground,
won't you please please help me?
When I was younger, so much younger
than today,
I never needed anybody's help in any
way,
but now these days are gone I'm not so
self assured,
now I find I've changed my mind I've
opened up the doors.
Help me if you can I'm feeling down,
and I do appreciate you being round,
help me get my feet back on the ground,
won't you please please help me? Help
me. Help me.

**"Help was great fun but it wasn't our
film. We were sort of guest stars.
It was fun, but basically as an idea for
a film it was a bit wrong for us."–Paul**

HELP

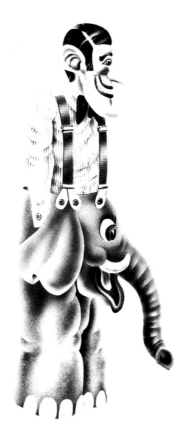

Sexy Sadie

Sexy Sadie what have you done.
You made a fool of everyone.
You made a fool of everyone.
Sexy Sadie ooh what have you done.
Sexy Sadie you broke the rules.
You laid it down for all to see.
You laid it down for all to see.
Sexy Sadie oooh you broke the rules.
One sunny day the world was waiting
for a lover.
She came along to turn on everyone.
Sexy Sadie the greatest of them all.
Sexy Sadie how did you know
The world was waiting just for you.
The world was waiting just for you.
Sexy Sadie you'll get yours yet.
However big you think you are.
However big you think you are.
Sexy Sadie oooh you'll get yours yet.
We gave her everything we owned just to
sit at her table
Just a smile would lighten everything
Sexy Sadie she's the latest and the greatest
of them all.
She made a fool of everyone
Sexie Sadie.
However big you think you are
Sexy Sadie.

"You'll get yours yet"—John

I am the walrus

I am he as you are he as you are me and
we are all together.
See how they run like pigs from a gun
see how they fly,
I'm crying.
Sitting on a cornflake – waiting for the
van to come.
Corporation teashirt, stupid bloody
Tuesday man you been a naughty boy you
let your face grow long.
I am the eggman oh, they are the eggmen –
Oh I am the walrus GOO GOO G'JOOB.
Mr. City policeman sitting pretty little
policeman in a row,
see how they fly like Lucy in the sky –
see how they run
I'm crying – I'm crying I'm crying.
Yellow matter custard dripping from a
dead dog's eye.
Crabalocker fishwife pornographic
priestess boy you been a naughty girl,
you let your knickers down.

I am the eggman oh, they are the eggmen –
Oh I am the walrus. GOO GOO G'JOOB.
Sitting in an English garden waiting for
the sun,
If the sun don't come, you get a tan from
standing in the English rain.
I am the eggman oh, they are the eggmen –
Oh, I am the walrus. G'JOOB, G'GOO,
G'JOOB.
Expert texpert choking smokers don't you
think the joker laughs at you?
Ha ha ha!
See how they smile, like pigs in a sty, see
how they snied.
I'm crying.
Semolina pilchards climbing up the Eiffel
Tower.
Elementary penguin singing Hare
Krishna man you should have seen them
kicking Edgar Allen Poe.
I am the eggman oh, they are the eggmen –
Oh I am the walrus GOO GOO GOO JOOB
GOO GOO GOO JOOB GOO GOO
GOOOOOOOOOOOJOOOOOB.

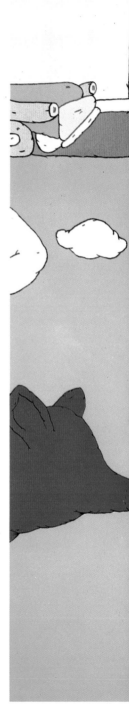

Nobody I know

Nobody I know could love me more than
you,
You can give me so much love it seems
untrue,
Listen to the bird who sings it to the tree,
And then when you've heard him see if
you agree,
Nobody I know could love you more than
me.
Ev'rywhere I go the sun comes shining
through,
Ev'ryone I know is sure it shines for you,
Even in my dreams I look into your eyes,
Suddenly it seems I've found a paradise,
Ev'rywhere I go the sun comes shining
through.
It means so much to be a part of a heart of
a wonderful one,
When other lovers are gone we'll live on,
We'll live on.
Even in my dreams I look into your eyes,
Suddenly it seems I've found a paradise,
Ev'rywhere I go the sun comes shining
through.
Nobody I know could love me more than
you,
You can give me so much love it seems
untrue,
Listen to the bird who sings it to the tree,
And then when you've heard him see if
you agree,
Nobody I know could love you more than
me.
Nobody I know could love you more than
me.

I am the walrus "All these financial takeovers and things—it's just like Monopoly"—John

She's leaving home

Wednesday morning at five o'clock as the day begins
silently closing her bedroom door
leaving the note that she hoped would say more
she goes downstairs to the kitchen
clutching her handkerchief
quietly turning the backdoor key
stepping outside she is free.
She (We gave her most of our lives)
is leaving (Sacrificed most of our lives)
home (We gave her everything money could buy)
she's leaving home after living alone
for so many years. Bye, bye.
Father snores as his wife gets into her dressing gown
picks up the letter that's lying there
standing alone at the top of the stairs
she breaks down and cries to her husband,
Daddy our baby's gone.
Why should she treat us to thoughtlessly
how could she do this to me.
She (We never thought of ourselves)
is leaving (Never a thought for ourselves)
home (We struggled hard all our lives to get by)
she's leaving home after living alone
for so many years. Bye, bye.
Friday morning at nine o'clock she is far away
waiting to keep the appointment she made
meeting a man from the motor trade.
She (What did we do that was wrong)
is leaving (We didn't know it was wrong)
home (Fun is the one thing that money can't buy)
something inside that was always denied
for so many years. Bye, bye.
She's leaving home bye bye.

"There was a Daily Mirror story about this girl who left home and her father said: 'We gave her everything, I don't know why she left home.' But he didn't give her that much, not what she wanted when she left home." – Paul

Hold me tight

It feels so right now, hold me tight,
Tell me I'm the only one,
And then I might,
Never be the lonely one.
So hold me tight, to-night, to-night,
It's you,
You you you—oo-oo—oo-oo.
Hold me tight,
Let me go on loving you,
To-night to-night,
Making love to only you,
So hold me tight, to-night, to-night,
It's you,
You you you—oo-oo—oo-oo.
Don't know what it means to hold you tight,
Being here alone tonight with you,
It feels so right now, feels so right now.
Hold me tight,
Tell me I'm the only one,
And then I might,
Never be the only one,
So hold me tight, to-night, to-night,
It's you,
You you you oo-oo—oo-oo.
Don't know what it means to hold you tight,
Being here alone tonight with you,
It feels so right now, feels so right now.
Hold me tight,
Let me go on loving you,
To-night to-night,
Making love to only you,
So hold me tight, to-night, to-night,
It's you,
You you you—oo-oo—oo-oo.

Don't let me down "I never signed a contract with the Beatles. I had given my word about what I intended to do, and that

s enough. I abided by the terms and no-one ever worried about me not signing it."—Brian Epstein

Don't let me down

Don't let me down
Don't let me down
Don't let me down
Don't let me down
Nobody ever loved me like she does
Ooh she does. Yes she does
And if somebody loved me
Like she do to me
Ooh she do me. Yes she does
Don't let me down
Don't let me down
Don't let me down
Don't let me down
I'm in love for the first time
Don't you know it's going to last
It's a love that lasts forever
It's a love that has no past
Don't let me down
Don't let me down
Don't let me down
Don't let me down
And from the first time that she really
done me
Ooh she done me. She done me good
I guess nobody ever really done me
Ooh she done me
She done me
She done me good
Don't let me down
Don't let me down
Don't let me down
Don't let me down

Doctor Robert

Ring my friend I said you'd call Doctor
Robert,
day or night he'll be there anytime at all,
Doctor Robert,
Doctor Robert, you're a new and better
man,
he helps you to understand,
he does ev'rything he can, Doctor Robert.
If you are down he'll pick you up, Doctor
Robert,
take a drink from his special cup, Doctor
Robert,
Doctor Robert, he's a man you must
believe,
helping ev'ry one in need,
no-one can succeed like Doctor Robert.
Well, well, well, you're feeling fine,
well, well, well, he'll make you, Doctor
Robert.
My friend works with the National
Health, Doctor Robert,
don't pay money just to see yourself with
Doctor Robert,
Doctor Robert, you're a new and better
man,
he helps you to understand,
he does ev'rything he can, Doctor Robert.
Well, well, well, you're feeling fine,
well, well, well, he'll make you Doctor
Robert.
Ring my friend I said you'd call
Doctor Robert.

**"Well, he's like a joke. There's some fellow in New York, and in the States
we'd hear people say 'You can get everything off him;
any pills you want . . .' That's what Dr. Roberts is all about, just a pill
doctor who sees you all right." – Paul**

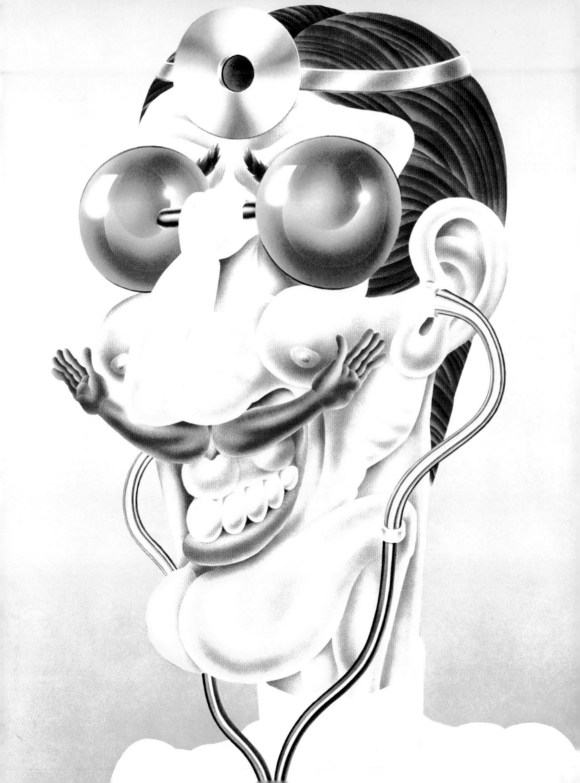

The above picture contains clues to thirteen Beatles' song titles; for example,
the eagle on John's eye refers to the line 'The eagle picks my eyes, the worm he licks my bones'
from Yer Blues. Can you find the other twelve titles? Answers on page 138.

Everybody's got something to hide except for me and my monkey

Come on come on come on come on
Come on is such a joy
Come on is such a joy
Come on take it easy
Come on take it easy.
Take it easy take it easy.
Everybody's got something to hide except
for me and my monkey.
The deeper you go the higher you fly.
The higher you fly the deeper you go.
So come on come on
Come on is such a joy
Come on is such a joy
Come on make it easy.
Come on make it easy.
Take it easy take it easy.
Everybody's got something to hide
except for me and my monkey.
Your inside is out and your outside is in.
Your outside is in and your inside is out.
So come on come on
Come on is such a joy
Come on is such a joy
Come on make it easy
Come on make it easy
Make it easy make it easy.
Everybody's got something to hide except
for me and my monkey.

**"I'm very shy, John is shy too."–
Yoko Ono**

Love you to

Each day just goes so fast,
I turn around, it's past,
you don't get time to hang a sign on me.
Love me while you can,
before I'm dead old man.
A life-time is so short,
a new one can't be bought,
but what you've got means such a lot to me.
Make love all day long,
make love singing songs.
Make love all day long,
make love singing songs.
There's people standing round,
who'll screw you in the ground,
they'll fill you in with all their sins,
you'll see.
I'll make love to you,
if you want me to.

**"I began to write more songs when I
had more time, especially when we
began to stop touring. Having Indian
things so much in my head it was
bound to come out."–George**

"The fans are really what it's all been about. And of course we like them. But there are times when we want to be left to hav⟨

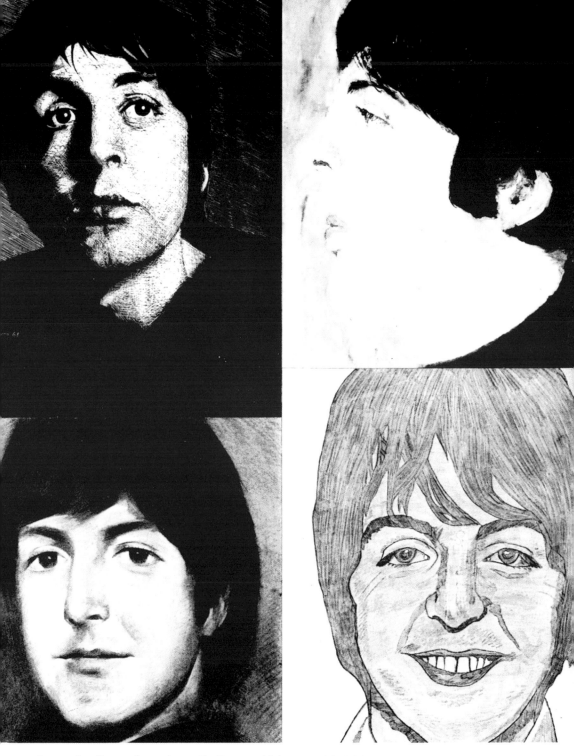

some privacy—when they can be a nuisance. But I suppose it's just part of the job."—Paul

I'm only sleeping

When I wake up early in the morning,
Lift my head, I'm still yawning.
When I'm in the middle of a dream,
Stay in bed, float up stream (float up
stream),
Please don't wake me, no, don't shake
me,
Leave me where I am, I'm only sleeping.
Everybody seems to think I'm lazy.
I don't mind, I think they're crazy
Running everywhere at such a speed,
Till they find there's no need (there's no
need),
Please don't spoil my day, I'm miles away,
And after all, I'm only sleeping.
Keeping an eye on the world going by my
window,
Taking my time, lying there and staring
at the ceiling,
Waiting for a sleepy feeling.
Please don't spoil my day, I'm miles
away,
And after all I'm only sleeping.
Keeping an eye on the world going by my
window,
Taking my time.
When I wake up early in the morning,
Lift my head, I'm still yawning,
When I'm in the middle of a dream,
Stay in bed, float up stream (float up
stream),
Please don't wake me, no, don't shake me,
Leave me where I am, I'm only sleeping.

Love me do

Love, love me do,
you know I love you.
I'll always be true
so please love me do, who ho love me do.
Love, love me do,
you know I love you.
I'll always be true
so please love me do, who ho love me do.
Someone to love, somebody new.
Someone to love, someone like you.
Love, love me do,
you know I love you.
I'll always be true
so please love me do, who ho love me do.
Love, love me do,
you know I love you.
I'll always be true
so please love me do, who ho love me do.

**"That's what we want to get back to—
simplicity. You can't have anything
simpler, yet more meaningful than
'love, love me—do.' That's just what
it means. I think I slagged off school
to write that one with John when we
first started."—Paul**

Yellow submarine
"I knew it would get connotations, but it really was a children's song. I just loved the idea of kids singing it." – Paul

94

I saw her standing there

Well, she was just seventeen,
You know what I mean,
And the way she looked was way beyond
compare,
So how could I dance with another,
oh when I saw her standing there.
Well she looked at me,
and I, I could see,
that before too long I'd fall in love with
her,
she wouldn't dance with another,
oh when I saw her dancing there.
Well my heart went zoom when I crossed
that room,
and I held her hand in mine.
Oh we danced through the night,
and we held each other tight,
and before too long I fell in love with her,
now I'll never dance with another,
oh when I saw her standing there.
Well my heart went zoom when I cross'd
that room,
and I held her hand in mine.
Oh we danced through the night,
and we held each other tight,
and before too long I fell in love with her,
now I'll never dance with another,
oh since I saw her standing there.
Oh since I saw her standing there.

Yellow submarine

In the town where I was born,
lived a man who sailed the sea,
and he told us of his life,
in the land of submarines.
So we sailed on to the sun,
till we found the sea of green,
and we lived beneath the waves,
in our yellow submarine.
We all live in a yellow submarine,
yellow submarine, yellow submarine,
we all live in a yellow submarine,
yellow submarine, yellow submarine.
And our friends are all aboard,
many more of them live next door,
and the band begins to play.
We all live in a yellow submarine,
yellow submarine, yellow submarine,
we all live in a yellow submarine,
yellow submarine, yellow submarine.
As we live a life of ease,
everyone of us has all we need,
sky of blue and sea of green,
in our yellow submarine.
We all live in a yellow submarine,
yellow submarine, yellow submarine,
we all live in a yellow submarine,
yellow submarine, yellow submarine.

"I was just thinking of nice words like Sergeant Pepper and Lonely Hearts Club, and they came together for no reason . . . They're a bit of a brass band in a way, but also a rock band because they've got the San Francisco thing."
—Paul

Sgt. Pepper's Lonely Hearts Club Band

It was twenty years ago today, that
Sgt. Pepper taught the band to play
they've been going in and out of style
but they're guaranteed to raise a smile.
So may I introduce to you
the act you've known for all these years,
Sgt. Pepper's Lonely Hearts Club Band.
We're Sgt. Pepper's Lonely Hearts Club
Band,
we hope you will enjoy the show,
We're Sgt. Pepper's Lonely Hearts Club
Band,
sit back and let the evening go.

Sgt. Pepper's lonely, Sgt. Pepper's
lonely,
Sgt. Pepper's Lonely Hearts Club Band.
It's wonderful to be here,
it's certainly a thrill.
You're such a lovely audience,
we'd like to take you home with us,
we'd love to take you home.
I don't really want to stop the show,
but I thought you might like to know,
that the singer's going to sing a song,
and he wants you all to sing along.
So may I introduce to you
the one and only Billy Shears
and Sgt. Pepper's Lonely Hearts Club
Band.

A hard day's night

It's been a hard day's night,
And I've been working like a dog,
It's been a hard day's night,
I should be sleeping like a log,
But when I get home to you,
I find that the things that you do,
Will make me feel alright.
You know I work all day,
To get you money to buy you things,
And it's worth it just to hear you say,
You're gonna give me ev'rything,
So why on earth should I moan,
Cos when I get you alone,
You know I feel okay.
When I'm home ev'rything seems to be
right,
When I'm home feeling you holding me
tight, tight, yeh.
It's been a hard day's night,
And I've been working like a dog,

It's been a hard day's night,
I should be sleeping like a log,
But when I get home to you,
I find the things that you do,
Will make me feel alright.
So why on earth should I moan,
'Cos when I get you alone,
You know I feel okay.
When I'm home ev'rything seems to be
right,
When I'm home feeling you holding me
tight, tight, yeh.
It's been a hard day's night,
And I've been working like a dog,
It's been a hard day's night,
I should be sleeping like a log,
But when I get home to you,
I find the things that you do,
Will make me feel alright.
You know I feel alright.
You know I feel alright.

"It wasn't so much that Brian Epstein discovered the Beatles but that the Beatles discovered Brian Epstein"–Paul

Baby, you're a rich man

How does it feel to be
One of the beautiful people?
Now that you know who you are
What do you want to be?
And have you travelled very far?
Far as the eye can see.
How does it feel to be
one of the beautiful people?
How often have you been there?
Often enough to know.
What did you see, when you were there?
Nothing that doesn't show.
Baby, you're a rich man,
Baby, you're a rich man,
Baby, you're a rich man too.
You keep all your money in a big brown
bag
inside a zoo.
What a thing to do.
Baby, you're a rich man,
Baby, you're a rich man,
Baby, you're a rich man too.
How does it feel to be
One of the beautiful people?
Tuned to A natural E
Happy to be that way.
Now that you've found another key
What are you going to play?
Baby, you're a rich man,
Baby, you're a rich man,
Baby, you're a rich man too.
You keep all your money in a big brown
bag
inside a zoo
What a thing to do.
Baby, you're a rich man . . .

"I want money just to be rich" – John

Yesterday

Yesterday,
all my troubles seemed so far away,
now it looks as though they're here to
stay,
oh, I believe in yesterday.
Suddenly,
I'm not half the man I used to be,
there's a shadow hanging over me,
oh, yesterday came suddenly.
Why she had to go I don't know,
she wouldn't say,
I said something wrong,
now I long for yesterday.
Yesterday,
love was such an easy game to play,
now I need a place to hide away,
oh, I believe in yesterday.
Why she had to go I don't know,
she wouldn't say,
I said something wrong,
now I long for yesterday.
Yesterday,
love was such an easy game to play,
now I need a place to hide away,
oh, I believe in yesterday.
Mm mm mm mm mm mm mm.

**"I woke up one morning and went to the piano.
And I just, you know, started playing it. And this tune came.
Because that's what happens you know,
they just come. But I couldn't think of any words
for it so originally I called it 'Scrambled Egg'. For a couple of
mornings that was what it was called. Then
I thought of 'Yesterday' and the words started to come
and we had a song." – Paul**

<u>Revolution</u> "The trouble is that so much of the pop and record business is being run by people who don't have a clue what it is about"—Paul

Revolution

You say you want a revolution
Well, you know
we all want to change the world.
You tell me that it's evolution,
Well, you know
we all want to change the world.
But when you talk about destruction,
Don't you know that you can count me
out.
Don't you know it's going to be alright,
Alright, alright.
You say you got a real solution
Well, you know
we'd all love to see the plan.
You ask me for a contribution,
Well, you know
we're doing what we can.
But if you want money for people with
minds that hate,
All I can tell you is brother you have to
wait.
Don't you know it's going to be alright,
Alright, alright.
You say you'll change a constitution
well, you know
we all want to change your head.
You tell me it's the institution,
well, you know
you better free your mind instead.
But if you go carrying pictures of
Chairman Mao,
You ain't going to make it with anyone
anyhow.
Don't you know it's going to be alright,
alright, alright.

Tell me what you see

If you let me take your heart I will prove
to you,
we will never be apart if I'm part of you,
open up your eyes now tell me what you
see,
it is no surprise now what you see is me.
Big and black the clouds may be time will
pass away,
if you put your trust in me I'll make bright
your day.
Look into these eyes now, tell me what
you see,
don't you realise now what you see is me.
Tell me what you see.
Listen to me one more time how can I get
through,
can't you try to see that I'm trying to get
to you,
open up your eyes now tell me what you
see,
it is no surprise now, what you see is me.
Tell me what you see.
Listen to me one more time how can I get
through.
Listen to me one more time, how can I get
through,
can't you try to see that I'm trying to get
to you,
open up your eyes now tell me what you
see,
it is no surprise what you see is me.

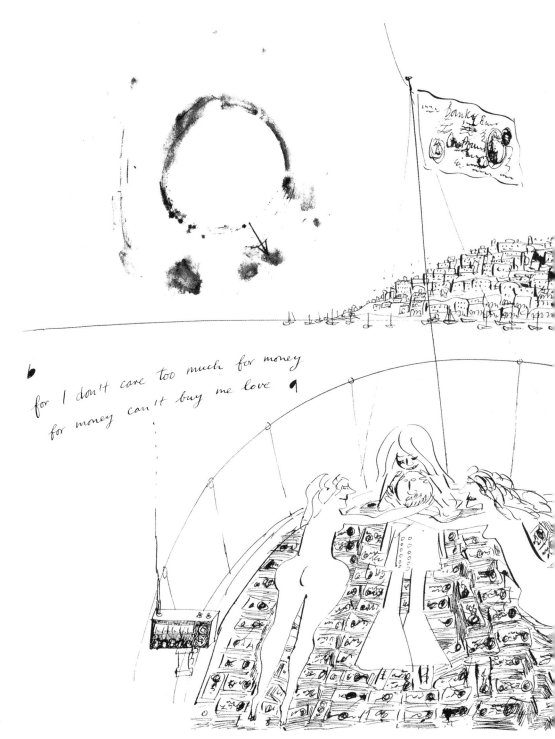

for I don't care too much for money
for money can't buy me love

Can't buy me love

Can't buy me love, love,
Can't buy me love.
I'll buy you a diamond ring my friend,
If it makes you feel alright,
I'll get you anything my friend,
If it makes you feel alright,
For I don't care too much for money,
For money can't buy me love.
I'll give you all I've got to give,
If you say you love me too,
I may not have a lot to give,
But what I've got I'll give to you,
For I don't care too much for money,
For money can't buy me love.
Can't buy me love, ev'rybody tells me so,
Can't buy me love, no, no, no, no.
Say you don't want no diamond ring,
And I'll be satisfied,
Tell me that you want those kind of
things,
That money just can't buy,
For I don't care too much for money,
For money can't buy me love.
Can't buy me love, ev'rybody tells me so,
Can't buy me love, no, no, no, no.
Say you don't want no diamond ring,
And I'll be satisfied,
Tell me that you want those kind of
things,
That money just can't buy
For I don't care too much for money,
For money can't buy me love.
Can't buy me love, ev'rybody tells me so,
Can't buy me love, no, no, no, no.
Can't buy me love, love,
Can't buy me love.

**"Personally, I think you can put any
interpretation you want on anything,
but when someone suggests that Can't
Buy Me Love is about a prostitute, I
draw the line. That's going too far."–
Paul**

John Glashan

The fool on the hill

Day after day, alone on a hill,
the man with the foolish grin is keeping
perfectly still.
But nobody wants to know him,
they can see that he's just a fool
and he never gives an answer.
But the fool on the hill sees the sun going
down
and the eyes in his head see the world
spinning round.
Well on the way, head in a cloud,
the man of a thousand voices talking
perfectly loud.
But nobody ever hears him
or the sound he appears to make
and he never seems to notice.
But the fool on the hill sees the sun
going down
and the eyes in his head see the world
spinning round.
And nobody seems to like him,
they can tell what he wants to do
and he never shows his feelings.
But the fool on the hill sees the sun going
down
and the eyes in his head see the world
spinning round.
He never listens to them,
he knows that they're the fools.
They don't like him.
The fool on the hill sees the sun going
down
and the eyes in his head see the world
spinning round.

**"We made a mistake, the Maharishi
is human. For a while we thought he
wasn't. We believe in meditation but
not the Maharishi and his scene.
We're finished with that bit of it."
—John**

The Inner Light

Without going out of my door
I can know all things on earth.
Without looking out of my window
I could know the ways of heaven.
The farther one travels,
The less one knows,
The less one knows.
Without going out of your door
You can know all things on earth.
Without looking out of your window
You can know the ways of heaven.
The farther one travels,
The less one knows,
The less one knows.
Arrive without travelling.
See all without looking.
(See all without looking).

**"George wrote this. Forget the
Indian music and listen to the
melody. Don't you think it's a
beautiful melody? It's really lovely."
—Paul**

108

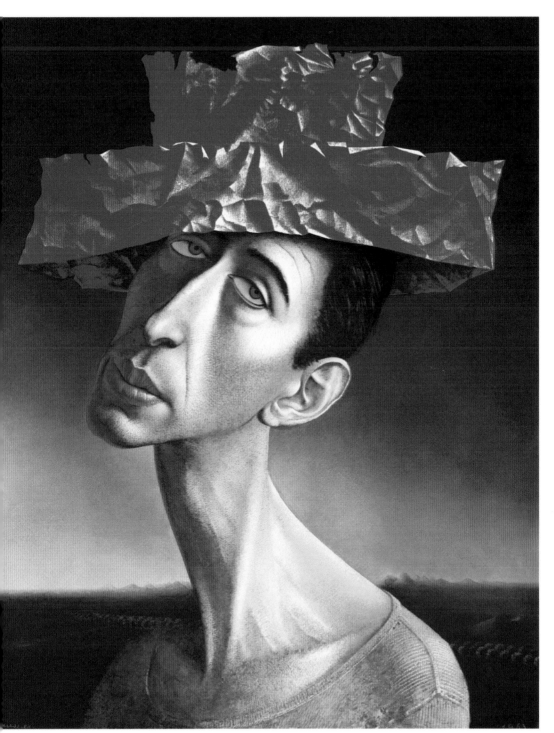

Oh George, and you're such a little man!!.

"Drop me a line with all the news, I've got a little bit behind The Times down here!"

Day tripper

Got a good reason for taking the easy
way out,
got a good reason for taking the easy
way out – now,
she was a day tripper,
one way ticket, yeh,
it took me so long to find out, and I found
out.
She's a big teaser, she took me half the
way there,
she's a big teaser, she took me half the
way there – now,
she was a day tripper,
one way ticket, yeh,
it took me so long to find out, and I found
out.
Tried to please her, she only played one
night stands,
tried to please her, she only played one
night stands – now,
she was a day tripper,
Sunday driver, yeh,
it took me so long to find out, and I found
out.
Day tripper, yeh.

"I can't get my winkle out
Isn't it a sin?
The more I try to get it out
The further it goes in!"

"You'd never believe the liberties the men take
down here. Perfect strangers too!"

"Oh, go on, Dick. The further
your in the nicer it feels"

SUPPOSE YOU FIND THIS RATHER FLAT
AFTER THE ALPS, MR. MOUNTWELL"

"KIDS HIMSELF HE'S A
GREAT LOVER—STARTS OFF WELL,
BUT CAN'T KEEP IT UP!"

Hello, Goodbye

You say yes, I say no,
You say stop, I say go, go, go.
Oh no.
You say goodbye and I say hello, hello,
hello.
I don't know why you say goodbye I say
hello, hello, hello.
I don't know why you say goodbye I say
hello.
I say high, you say low.
You say why and I say I don't know.
Oh no.
You say goodbye and I say hello, hello,
hello.
I don't know why you say goodbye I say
hello, hello, hello.
I don't know why you say goodbye I say
hello.
Why, why, why, why, why, why, do you
say goodbye, goodbye, bye, bye.
Oh no.
You say goodbye and I say hello, hello,
hello.
I don't know why you say goodbye I say
hello, hello, hello.
I don't know why you say goodbye I say
hello.
You say yes, I say no (I say yes but I may
mean no)
You say stop and I say go, go, go (I can
stall till it's time to go)
Oh, oh no.
You say goodbye and I say hello, hello,
hello.
I don't know why you say goodbye I say
hello, hello, hello.
I don't know why you say goodbye I say
hello, hello, hello.
I don't know why you say goodbye I say
hello, hello, hello.
hello, hello, hello.
Hela, heba, helloa.

**"Those in the cheaper seats clap. The
rest of you rattle your jewellery."
–John, at the Royal Variety
Performance, November 15, 1963**

Paperback writer

Paperback writer, Paperback writer,
Dear Sir or Madam will you read my
book,
It took me years to write will you take a
look,
Based on a novel by a man named Lear,
And I need a job,
So I want to be a paperback writer,
Paperback writer.
It's a dirty story of a dirty man,
And his clinging wife doesn't understand.
His son is working for the Daily Mail,
It's a steady job,
But he wants to be a paperback writer,
Paperback writer.
It's a thousand pages give or take a few,
I'll be writing more in a week or two,
I can make it longer if you like the style,
I can change it round,
And I want to be a paperback writer,
Paperback writer.
If you really like it you can have the rights,
It could make a million for you overnight,
If you must return it you can send it here,
But I need a break,
And I want to be a paperback writer,
Paperback writer.

If I fell

If I fell in love with you would you
promise to be true,
And help me understand?
'Cos I've been in love before, and I found
that love was more,
Than just holding hands.
If I give my heart to you,
I must be sure from the very start,
That you would love me more than her.
If I trust in you, oh please,
Don't run and hide,
If I love you too, oh please don't hurt my
pride like her.
'Cos I couldn't stand the pain,
And I would be sad if our new love was in
vain.
So I hope you see,
That I would love to love you,
And that she will cry when she learns we
are two.
'Cos I couldn't stand the pain,
And I would be sad if our new love was
in vain.
So I hope you see,
That I would love to love you,
And that she will cry when she learns we
are two.
If I fell in love with you.

Paperback writer

Paperback writer, Paperback writer

Dear Sir or Madam will you read my book,
it took me years to write will you take a look,
based on a novel by a man named Lear,
and I need a job,
So I want to be a paperback writer,
paperback writer

It's a dirty story of a dirty man,
and his clinging wife doesn't understand.
His son is working for the Daily Mail,
it's a steady job,
but he wants to be a paperback writer,
paperback writer

It's a thousand pages give or take a few,
I'll be writing more in a week or two.
I can make it longer if you like the style,
I can change it round,
and I want to be a paperback writer,
paperback writer

If you really like it you can have the rights,
It could make a million for you overnight.
If you must return it you can send it here,
but I need a break,
and I want to be a paperback writer,
paperback writer

FOLON

114

Paperback writer
"Everyone gets
down on their
knees and
grovels a bit"–
Paul   115

Think for yourself "It was just a beautiful idea of John's to plant an acorn, and the only way you can better John is by copying him exactly." – Yoko Ono

Think for yourself

I've got a word or two
to say about the things that you do,
you're telling all those lies,
about the good things that we can have if
we close our eyes.
Do what you want to do,
and go where you're going to,
think for yourself,
'cos I won't be there with you.
I left you far behind
the ruins of the life that you had in mind.
And though you still can't see,
I know your mind's made up, you're
gonna cause more misery.
Do what you want to do,
and go where you're going to,
think for yourself,
'cos I won't be there with you.
Although your mind's opaque,
try thinking more,
if just for your own sake.
the future still looks good,
and you've got time to rectify
all the things that you should.
Do what you want to do,
and go where you're going to,
think for yourself,
'cos I won't be there with you.
Do what you want to do,
and go where you're going to,
think for yourself,
'cos I won't be there with you.
Think for yourself,
'cos I won't be there with you.

You won't see me

When I call you up your line's engaged.
I have had enough, so act your age,
we have lost the time that was so hard to
find,
and I will lose my mind,
if you won't see me, you won't see me.
I don't know why you should want to
hide,
but I can't get through my hands are tied,
I won't want to stay I don't have much to
say,
but I can turn away,
and you won't see me, you won't see me.
Time after time you refuse to even listen,
I wouldn't mind if I knew what I was
missing.
Though the days are few they're filled
with tears,
and since I lost you it feels like years,
yes it seems so long girl since you've
been gone,
I just can't go on,
if you won't see me, you won't see me.
Time after time you refuse to even listen,
I wouldn't mind if I knew what I was
missing.
Though the days are few they're filled
with tears,
and since I lost you it feels like years,
yes it seems so long girl since you've
been gone,
I just can't go on,
if you won't see me, you won't see me.
Oo–Oo–

Yer blues

Yes I'm lonely wanna die
Yes I'm lonely wanna die
If I ain't dead already.
Ooh girl you know the reason why.
In the morning wanna die.
In the evening wanna die.
If I ain't dead already.
Ooh girl you know the reason why.
My mother was of the sky.
My father was of the earth.
But I am of the universe
And you know what it's worth.
I'm lonely wanna die.
If I ain't dead already.
Ooh girl you know the reason why.
The eagle picks my eye.
The worm he licks my bone.
I feel so suicidal
Just like Dylan's Mr. Jones.
Lonely wanna die.
If I ain't dead already.
Ooh girl you know the reason why.
Black cloud crossed my mind.
Blue mist round my soul.
Feel so suicidal
Even hate my rock and roll.
Wanna die yeah wanna die.
If I ain't dead already.
Ooh girl you know the reason why.

**"We're more popular than
Jesus Christ now. I don't know
which will go first. Rock and
roll or Christianity. Jesus was
all right, but his disciples were
thick and ordinary. It's them
twisting it that ruins it for
me."—John**

There's a place

There, there's a place,
Where I can go,
When I feel low,
When I feel blue,
And it's my mind,
And there's no time,
When I'm alone.
I think of you,
And things you do,
Go round my head,
The things you've said,
Like I love only you.
In my mind there's no sorrow,
Don't you know that it's so.
There'll be no sad tomorrow,
Don't you know that it's so.
There, there's a place,
Where I can go,
When I feel low,
When I feel blue,
And it's my mind,
And there's no time,
When I'm alone.
There, there's a place,
There's a place.

**"It was just like Butlin's."
—Ringo, after returning
from meditating
at Rishikesh in the
Himalayas**

Tomorrow never knows

Turn off your mind relax and float
down-stream,
it is not dying, it is not dying,
lay down all thought surrender to the
void,
it is shining, it is shining.
That you may see the meaning of within,
it is speaking, it is speaking,
that love is all and love is ev'ryone,
it is knowing, it is knowing.
When ignorance and haste may mourn
the dead,
it is believing, it is believing.
But listen to the colour of your dreams,
it is not living, it is not living.
Or play the game existence to the end.
Of the beginning, of the beginning.
Of the beginning. Of the beginning.

**"Often the backing I think of early on
never comes off. With 'Tomorrow
Never Knows' I'd imagine in my head
that in the background you would hear
thousands of monks chanting.
That was impractical of course and we
did something different. I should have
tried to get near my original idea, the
monks singing, I realise now that was
what it wanted." – John**

I'm looking through you

I'm looking through you, where did you
go?
I thought I knew you, what did I know?
You don't look different, but you have
changed,
I'm looking through you, you're not the
same.
Your lips are moving, I cannot hear,
your voice is soothing but the words
aren't clear.
You don't sound different, I've learnt
the game,
I'm looking through you, you're not the
same.
Why, tell me why did you not treat me
right?
Love has a nasty habit of disappearing
overnight,
you're thinking of me the same old way,
you were above me, but not today.
The only difference is you're down there.
I'm looking through you and you're
nowhere.
Why, tell me why did you not treat me
right?
Love has a nasty habit of disappearing
overnight,
I'm looking through you, where did you
go?
I thought I knew you, what did I know?
You don't look different, but you have
changed,
I'm looking through you, you're not the
same.
Yeh, I tell you you've changed.

121

"Draw the curtains so they can't see us. We've only come away for a few days to make a film, and we have to put up with a

his."—George, when fans laid siege to the hotel where the Beatles were staying during the filming of Magical Mystery Tour

Honey pie

She was a working girl
North of England way.
Now she's hit the big time
In the U.S.A.
And if she could only hear me
This is what I'd say.
Honey pie you are making me crazy.
I'm in love but I'm lazy.
So won't you please come home.
Oh honey pie my position is tragic.
Come and show me the magic
of your Hollywood song.
You became a legend of the silver screen
And now the thought of meeting you
Makes me weak in the knee.
Oh honey pie you are driving me frantic.
Sail across the Atlantic
To be where you belong.
Will the wind that blew her boat
Across the sea
Kindly send her sailing back to me.
Honey pie you are making me crazy.
I'm in love but I'm lazy.
So won't you please come home.

**"I think people think I'm the cute
one."–Paul, on the David Frost
television show**

I want to hold your hand

Oh yeh, I'll tell you something,
I think you'll understand,
then I'll say that something,
I wanna hold your hand,
I wanna hold your hand,
I wanna hold your hand.
Oh please say to me
you'll let me be your man,
and please say to me
you'll let me hold your hand,
now let me hold your hand,
I wanna hold your hand.
And when I touch you
I feel happy inside,
it's such a feeling
that my love I can't hide,
I can't hide, I can't hide.
Yeh, you got that something,
I think you'll understand,
when I feel that something,
I wanna hold your hand,
I wanna hold your hand,
I wanna hold your hand.
And when I touch you
I feel happy inside,
it's such a feeling
that my love I can't hide,
I can't hide, I can't hide.
Yeh, you got that something,
I think you'll understand,
when I feel that something,
I wanna hold your hand,
I wanna hold your hand,
I wanna hold your hand.

**"The submediant switches from C
Major into A flat Major and to a lesser
extent mediant ones (e.g. I want to hold
your hand) are the trademark of
Lennon and McCartney songs."–
The Times music critic**

Colette Portal

"I think it was Miss Daisy
Hawkins originally—
but I wanted a name that
was more real. The
thought just came: 'Eleanor
Rigby picks up the
rice and lives in a dream.'
She didn't make it with
anyone, she didn't
even look as if she was
going to." —Paul

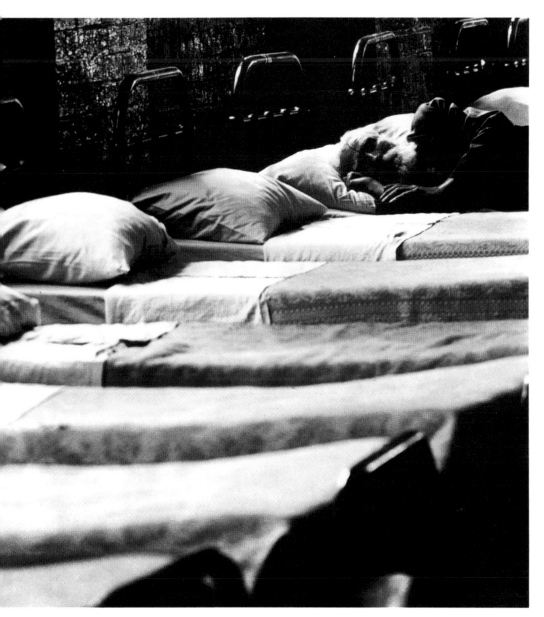

Eleanor Rigby

Ah, look at all the lonely people.
Ah, look at all the lonely people.
Eleanor Rigby picks up the rice in the
church where a wedding has been,
lives in a dream.
Waits at the window, wearing the face
that she keeps in a jar by the door,
Who is it for?
All the lonely people, where do they all
come from?

All the lonely people, where do they all
belong?
Father McKenzie, writing the words of a
sermon that no-one will hear,
No-one comes near.
Look at him working, darning his socks in
the night when there's nobody there,
What does he care?
All the lonely people, where do they all
come from?
All the lonely people, where do they all
belong?

Ah, look at all the lonely people.
Ah, look at all the lonely people.
Eleanor Rigby died in the church and was
buried along with her name.
Nobody came.
Father McKenzie, wiping the dirt from
his hands as he walks from the grave.
No-one was saved.
All the lonely people, where do they all
come from?
All the lonely people, where do they all
belong?

127

With a little help from my friends

What would you do if I sang out of tune,
would you stand up and walk out on me.
Lend me your ears and I'll sing you a
song,
and I'll try not to sing out of key.
I get by with a little help from my friends,
I get high with a little help from my
friends,
I'm gonna try with a little help from my
friends.
What do I do when my love is away.
(Does it worry you to be alone)
How do you feel by the end of the day
(are you sad because you're on your own)
no I get by with a little help from my
friends,
I get high with a little help from my
friends,
Oh I'm gonna try with a little help from
my friends.
Do you need anybody,
I need somebody to love.
Could it be anybody
I want somebody to love.
Would you believe in a love at first sight,
yes I'm certain that it happens all the
time.
What do you see when you turn out the
light,
I can't tell you, but I know it's mine.
Oh I get by with a little help from my
friends.
I get high with a little help from my
friends,
Oh I'm gonna try with a little help from
my friends.
Do you need anybody,
I just need somebody to love,
Could it be anybody,
I want somebody to love. Oh
I get by with a little help from my friends,
Mm I'm gonna try with a little help from
my friends,
Oh I get high with a little help from my
friends,
Yes I get by with a little help from my
friends.

**"You know I'm not very good at
singing because I haven't got a great
range. So they write songs for me that
are pretty low and not too hard."—
Ringo**

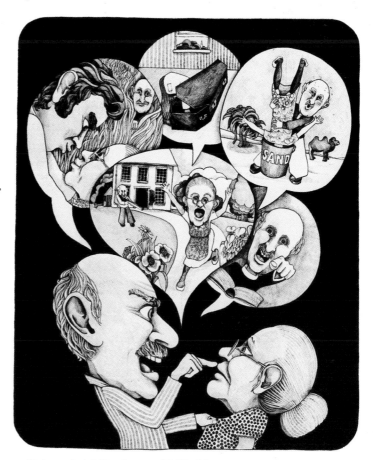

"I always hated 'Run for your life.' "—John

Run for your life

I'd rather see you dead, little girl,
than to be with another man.
You'd better keep your head, little girl,
or I won't know where I am.
You'd better run for your life
if you can, little girl,
hide your head in the sand, little girl.
Catch you with another man,
that's the end—ah, little girl.
Well you know that I'm a wicked guy,
and I was born with a jealous mind,
and I can't spend my whole life tryin',
just to make you toe the line.
You'd better run for your life
if you can, little girl,
hide your head in the sand, little girl,
catch you with another man,

that's the end—ah, little girl.
Let this be a sermon,
I mean everything I said,
baby, I'm determined,
and I'd rather see you dead.
You'd better run for your life
if you can, little girl,
hide your head in the sand, little girl,
catch you with another man,
that's the end—ah, little girl.
I'd rather see you dead, little girl,
than to be with another man,
you'd better keep your head, little girl,
or I won't know where I am.
You'd better run for your life,
if you can, little girl,
hide your head in the sand, little girl,
catch you with another man,
that's the end—ah, little girl.

LONDON: TEENAGE FANS SOB AT WEDDING OF
BEATLE PAUL McCARTNEY, MOST BELOVED MEM
FOURSOME, TO U.S. PHOTOGRAPHER LINDA EA

Baby's in black

Oh dear, what can I do?
Baby's in black and I'm feeling blue,
Tell me, oh what can I do?
She thinks of him and so she dresses in
black,
And though he'll never come back, she's
dressed in black.
Oh dear, what can I do?
Baby's in black and I'm feeling blue,
Tell me, oh what can I do?
I think of her, but she only thinks of him,
And though it's only a whim, she thinks
of him.
Oh how long will it take,
Till she sees the mistake she has made?
Dear, what can I do?
Baby's in black and I'm feeling blue,
Tell me, oh what can I do?
Oh how long will it take,
Till she sees the mistake she has made?
Dear, what can I do?
Baby's in black and I'm feeling blue,
Tell me, oh what can I do?
She thinks of him and so she dresses in
black,
And though he'll never come back, she's
dressed in black.
Oh dear, what can I do?
Baby's in black and I'm feeling blue,
Tell me, oh what can I do?

Your Mother should know

Let's all get up and dance to a song
that was a hit before your Mother was
born
Though she was born a long long time ago
your Mother should know—your Mother
should know
sing it again.
Lift up your hearts and sing me a song
that was a hit before your Mother was
born
Though she was born a long long time ago
your Mother should know—your Mother
should know
your Mother should know—your Mother
should know
sing it again.
Though she was born a long long time ago
your Mother should know—your Mother
should know
your Mother should know—your Mother
should know
your Mother should know—your Mother
should know.

Blue Jay Way

There's a fog upon L.A.
And my friends have lost their way
we'll be over soon they said
now they've lost themselves instead.
Please don't be long please don't you be
very long
please don't be long or I may be asleep
well it only goes to show
and I told them where to go
ask a policeman on the street
there's so many there to meet
please don't be long please don't you be
very long
please don't be long or I may be asleep
now it's past my bed I know
and I'd really like to go
soon will be the break of day
sitting here in Blue Jay Way
please don't be long please don't you be
very long
please don't be long or I may be asleep.
Please don't be long please don't you be
very long
please don't be long
please don't be long please don't you be
very long
please don't be long
please don't be long please don't you be
very long
please don't be long
don't be long—don't be long—don't be
long
don't be long—don't be long—don't be
long

**"Derek got held up. He rang up to say
he'd be late. I told him on the phone
that the house was in Blue Jay Way. He
said he could find it okay, he could
always ask a cop."—George**

133

Rain

If the rain comes they run and hide their heads.
They might as well be dead,
If the rain comes, if the rain comes.
When the sun shines they slip into the shade,
And sip their lemonade,
When the sun shines, when the sun shines.
Rain, I don't mind,
Shine, the weather's fine.
I can show you that when it starts to rain,
Everything's the same,
I can show you, I can show you.
Rain, I don't mind,
Shine, the weather's fine.
Can you hear me that when it rains and shines,
It's just a state of mind,
Can you hear me, can you hear me?

**"On the end of 'Rain' you hear me
singing it backwards. We'd done
the main thing at EMI and the habit
was then to take the song home and
see what you thought a little extra
gimmick or what the guitar piece
would be. So I got home about five in
the morning, stoned out of my head,
I staggered up to my tape recorder
and I put it on, but it came out
backwards, and I was in a trance in
the earphones, what is it, what is it.
It's too much, you know, and I really
wanted the whole song backwards
almost, and that was it. So we tagged it
on the end. I just happened to have the
tape on the wrong way round, it just
came out backwards, it just blew me
mind. The voice sounds like an old
Indian."—John, Rolling Stone**

All you need is love

Love, love, love, love, love, love, love, love, love.
There's nothing you can do that can't be done.
Nothing you can sing that can't be sung.
Nothing you can say but you can learn how to play the game
It's easy.
There's nothing you can make that can't be made.
No one you can save that can't be saved.
Nothing you can do but you can learn how to be you in time
It's easy.
All you need is love, all you need is love,
All you need is love, love, love is all you need.
Love, love, love, love, love, love, love, love.
All you need is love, all you need is love,
All you need is love, love, love is all you need.
There's nothing you can know that isn't known.
Nothing you can see that isn't shown.
Nowhere you can be that isn't where you're meant to be.
It's easy.
All you need is love, all you need is love,
all you need is love, love, love is all you need.
All you need is love (all together now)
All you need is love (everybody)
All you need is love, love, love is all you need.

**"We're going to send two acorns for
peace to every world leader from John
and Yoko. Perhaps if they plant them
and watch them grow they may get the
idea into their heads."—John**

"Klaus (Voorman) had
a harmonium in his house,
which I hadn't played before.
I was doodling on it, playing
to amuse myself, when
'Within You' started to come.
The tune came first then I got the first
sentence. It came
out of what we'd been doing
that evening."—George

Within you without you

We were talking—about the space
between us all
And the people—who hide themselves
behind a wall of illusion
Never glimpse the truth—then it's far too
late—when they pass away.
We were talking—about the love we all
could share—when we find it
to try our best to hold it there—with our
love
With our love—we could save the world—
if they only knew.
Try to realise it's all within yourself
no-one else can make you change
And to see you're really only very small,
and life flows on within you and without
you.
We were talking—about the love that's
gone so cold and the people,
who gain the world and lose their soul—
they don't know—they can't see—are you
one of them?
When you've seen beyond yourself—
then you may find peace of mind, is
waiting there—
And the time will come when you see
we're all one,
and life flows on within you and without
you.

I want to tell you

I want to tell you,
my head is filled with things to say,
when you're here,
all those words they seem to slip away.
When I get near you,
the games begin to drag me down,
it's alright,
I'll make you maybe next time around.
But if I seem to act unkind,
it's only me, it's not my mind,
that is confusing things.
I want to tell you,
I feel hung up and I don't know why,
I don't mind, I could wait for ever,
I've got time.
Sometimes I wish I knew you well,
then I could speak my mind and tell you
maybe you'd understand.
I want to tell you.
I feel hung up and I don't know why,
I don't mind, I could wait for ever,
I've got time. I've got time.

**"I mean we're human too. I do get
hurt when they attack Yoko or say
she's ugly or something."—John**

137

1. When I'm sixty-four
'You can knit a sweater by the fireside.'
2. Yer blues
'The eagle picks my eye. The worm he licks my bone.'
3. The continuing story of Bungalow Bill
'He went out tiger hunting with his elephant and gun
In case of accidents he always took his mom.'

4. With a little help from my friends
'Lend me your ears and I'll sing you a song.'
5. Love you to
'There's people standing round, who'll screw you in the ground.'
6. Strawberry Fields forever
7. Lucy in the sky with diamonds
'Picture yourself in a boat on a river . . . Cellophane

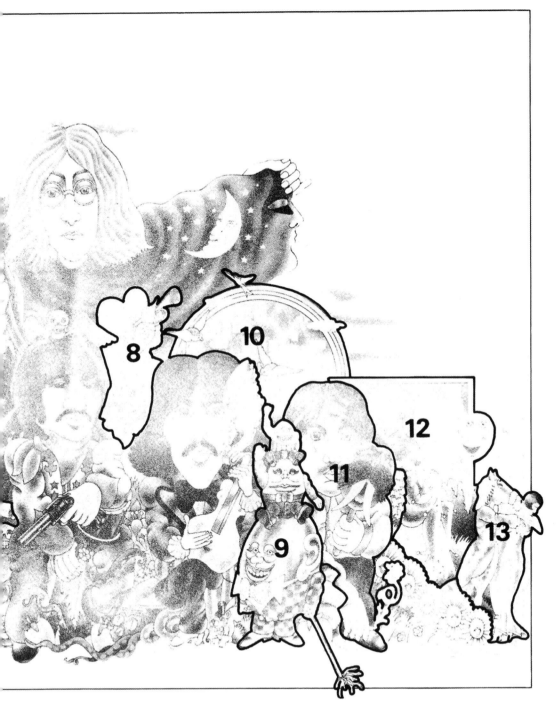

flowers of yellow and green, towering over your head.'
8. Sgt. Pepper's Lonely Hearts Club Band
9. I am the walrus
'. . . they are the eggmen.'
10. Penny Lane
'. . . beneath the blue suburban skies.'

11. Glass onion
'Well here's another clue for you all the walrus was Paul.'
12. The fool on the hill
'But the fool on the hill sees the sun going down.'
13. Being for the benefit of Mr. Kite!
'. . . and of course Henry the Horse dances the waltz!'

Birthday

You say it's your birthday.
It's my birthday too—yeah.
They say it's your birthday.
We're gonna have a good time.
I'm glad it's your birthday
Happy birthday to you.
Yes we're going to a party party
Yes we're going to a party party
Yes we're going to a party party.
I would like you to dance—Birthday
Take a cha-cha-cha-chance—Birthday
I would like you to dance—Birthday
dance
You say it's your birthday.
Well it's my birthday too—yeah.
You say it's your birthday.
We're gonna have a good time.
I'm glad it's your birthday
Happy birthday to you.

"I was 62 the day they had the premiere of 'A Hard Day's Night' and we all went to the Dorchester. Then Paul handed me a big parcel—and I opened it and it was a picture of a horse. So I said 'Very nice'—but I thought, what do I want with a picture of a horse? Then Paul must have seen my face because he said 'It's not just a picture dad. I've bought you the bloody horse.' "—James McCartney

Penny Lane

In Penny Lane there is a barber showing photographs
of ev'ry head he's had the pleasure to know.
And all the people that come and go
stop and say "Hello".
On the corner is a banker with a motorcar,
the little children laugh at him behind his back.
And the banker never wears a mac
In the pouring rain—very strange.
Penny Lane is in my ears and in my eyes,
there beneath the blue suburban skies
I sit, and meanwhile back
In Penny Lane there is a fireman with an hourglass
and in his pocket is a portrait of the Queen.
He likes to keep his fire engine clean,
it's a clean machine.
Penny Lane is in my ears and in my eyes,
a four of fish and finger pies
in summer meanwhile back
Behind the shelter in the middle of the roundabout
The pretty nurse is selling poppies from a tray.
And though she feels as if she's in a play
she is anyway.
In Penny Lane, the barber shaves another customer, we see the banker sitting waiting for a trim
and then the fireman rushes in
from the pouring rain—very strange.
Penny Lane is in my ears and in my eyes,
there beneath the blue suburban skies
I sit, and meanwhile back
Penny Lane is in my ears and in my eyes,
there beneath the blue suburban skies . . .
Penny Lane!

"Penny Lane is a bus roundabout in Liverpool; and there is a barber's shop showing photographs of every head he's had the pleasure to know—no that's not true, they're just photos of hairstyles, but all the people who come and go stop and say hello. It's part fact, part nostalgia for a place which is a great place, blue suburban skies as we remember it, and it's still there."—Paul

141

Lovely Rita

Lovely Rita meter maid.
Lovely Rita meter maid.
Lovely Rita meter maid.
Nothing can come between us,
when it gets dark I tow your heart away.
Standing by a parking meter,
when I caught a glimpse of Rita,
filling in a ticket in her little white book.
In a cap she looked much older,
and the bag across her shoulder
made her look a little like a military man.
Lovely Rita meter maid,
may I inquire discreetly,
when you are free,
to take some tea with me.
Took her out and tried to win her,
had a laugh and over dinner,
told her I would really like to see her
again,
got the bill and Rita paid it,
took her home and nearly made it,
sitting on a sofa with a sister or two.
Oh, lovely Rita meter maid,
where would I be without you.
Give us a wink and make me think of you.

**"I was bopping about on the piano in
Liverpool when someone told me that
in America they call parking-meter
women meter-maids. I thought that
was great and it got to be Rita Meter
Maid and then Lovely Rita Meter Maid
and I was thinking that it should be a
hate song . . . but then I thought it
would be better to love her, and if she
was very freaky too, like a military
man, with a bag on her shoulder. A
foot stomper, but nice."—Paul**

peter max

Glass onion

I told you about strawberry fields.
You know the place where nothing is
real.
Well here's another place you can go
Where everything flows.
Looking through the bent backed tulips
To see how the other half live
Looking through a glass onion.
I told you about the walrus and me—man.
You know that we're as close as can be—
man.
Well here's another clue for you all
The walrus was Paul.
Standing on the cast iron shore—yeah.
Lady Madonna trying to make ends meet
—yeah.
Looking through a glass onion.
Oh yeah oh yeah oh yeah
Looking through a glass onion.
I told you about the fool on the hill.
I tell you man he living there still.
Well here's another place you can be.
Listen to me.
Fixing a hole in the ocean
Trying to make a dove-tail joint—yeah
Looking through a glass onion.

Get back

(1)
Jojo was a man who thought he was a
loner
But he knew it couldn't last.
Jojo left his home in Tucson, Arizona
For some California Grass.
Get back, get back, get back to where you
once belonged
Get back, get back.
Get back to where you once belonged.
Get back Jojo. Go home
Get back, get back.
Back to where you once belonged
Get back, get back.
Back to where you once belonged.
Get back Jo.
(2)
Sweet Loretta Martin thought she was a
woman
But she was another man
All the girls around her say she's got it
coming
But she gets it while she can.
Get back, get back.
Get back to where you once belonged.
Get back, get back.
Get back to where you once belonged.
Get back Loretta. Go home
Get back, get back.
Get back to where you once belonged
Get back, get back.
Get back to where you once belonged.
Get back Loretta
Your mother's waiting for you
Wearing her high-heel shoes
And her low-neck sweater
Get on home Loretta
Get back, get back.
Get back to where you once belonged.

Get back
"We were sitting in the
studio and we made it up out of thin
air . . . we started to write words there
and then . . . when we finished it, we
recorded it at Apple Studios and made
it into a song to roller-coast by."—Paul

145

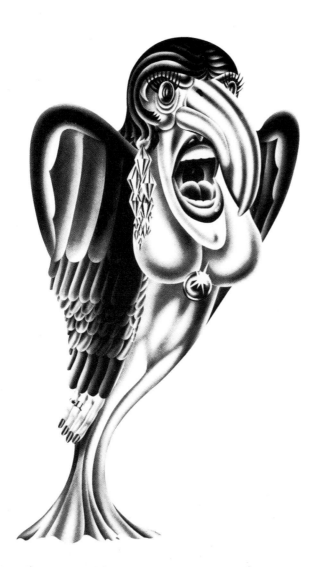

And your bird can sing

You tell me that you've ev'ry thing you
want,
And your bird can sing,
But you don't get me,   You don't get me.
You say you've seen seven wonders,
And your bird is green,
But you can't see me,   You can't see me.
When your prized possessions start to
wear you down,
Look in my direction I'll be round,
I'll be round.
When your bird is broken will it bring
you down?
You may be awoken I'll be round,
I'll be round.
Tell me that you've heard ev'ry sound
there is,
And your bird can swing,
But you can't hear me,
You can't hear me.

Dear Prudence

Dear Prudence, won't you come out to
play.
Dear Prudence, greet the brand new day.
The sun is up, the sky is blue.
It's beautiful and so are you.
Dear Prudence won't you come out to
play?
Dear Prudence open up your eyes.
Dear Prudence see the sunny skies.
The wind is low the birds will sing
That you are part of everything.
Dear Prudence won't you open up your
eyes?
Look around round
Look around round round
Look around.
Dear Prudence let me see you smile.
Dear Prudence like a little child.
The clouds will be a daisy chain.
So let me see you smile again.
Dear Prudence won't you let me see you
smile?

Hey bulldog

Sheep dog standing in the rain.
Bull frog doing it again.
Some kind of happiness is measured out in
miles.
What makes you think you're something
special when you smile.
Child-like yeah, no one understands.
Jack-knife in your sweaty hands.
Some kind of innocence is measured out
in years.
You don't know what it's like to listen to
your fears.
You can talk to me,
You can talk to me,
You can talk to me,
If you're lonely you can talk to me (yeah!)
Big man walking in the park
Wigwam frightened of the dark
Some kind of solitude is measured out in
you.
You think you know it but you haven't got
a clue.
You can talk to me,
You can talk to me,
You can talk to me,
If you're lonely you can talk to me (yeah!)
Hey bulldog, hey bulldog, hey bulldog
Hey, bulldog, Woof!
wha'd'ya say?
I said woof!
d'y' know any more?
Wowu-wa Ah!

**"Paul said we should do a real song in
the studio, to save wasting time.
Could I whip one off? I had a few
words at home so I brought them in."**–
John, on how 'Hey bulldog' was
recorded

It's all too much

It's all too much
It's all too much
When I look into your eyes
Your love is there for me
And the more I go inside
The more there is to see.
It's all too much for me to take
The love that's shining all around you
Everywhere it's what you make
for us to take it's all too much.
Floating down the stream of time
From life to life with me
Makes no difference where you are
or where you'd like to be.
It's all too much for me to take
The love that's shining all around here.
All the world is birthday cake
so take a piece but not too much.
Sail me on a silver sun
Where I know that I am free
Show me that I'm everywhere
and get me home for tea.
It's all too much for me to take
There's plenty there for everybody
The more you give the more you get
The more it is and it's too much.
It's all too much for me to see
The love that's shining all around you
The more I learn the less I know
But what I do is all too much.
It's all too much for me to take
The love that's shining all around you
Everywhere it's what you make
for us to take it's all too much.
It's much, it's much.
It's too much
Ah! it's too much
You are too much ah!
We are dead ah!
Too much, too much, too much-a. FADE

**"George is turning out songs like Soft
Mick these days."**–John

All Together Now

One, two, three, four,
Can I have a little more,
Five, six, seven, eight, nine, ten,
I love you.
A, B, C, D,
Can I bring my friend to tea,
E, F, G, H, I, J,
I love you.
Bom bom bom bom-pa bom
Sail the ship bom-pa bom
Chop the tree bom-pa bom
Skip the rope bom-pa bom
Look at me.
All together now, all together now,
All together now, all together now,
Black, white, green, red,
Can I take my friend to bed,
Pink, brown, yellow, orange and blue,
I love you.
All together now, all together now,
All together now, all together now,
Bom bom bom bom bom-pa bom
Sail the ship bom-pa bom
Chop the tree bom-pa bom
Skip the rope bom-pa bom
Look at me.
All together now, all together now,
All together now, all together now,
All together now!

**"The thing is, we're all really the
same person. We're just four parts of
the one."**–Paul

P.S. I love you

As I write this letter, send my love to you,
remember that I'll always be in love with
you.
Treasure these few words till we're
together
keep all my love forever.
P.S. I love you, you, you, you.
I'll be coming home again to you love,
until the day I do love.
P.S. I love you, you, you, you.
As I write this letter, send my love to you,
remember that I'll always be in love with
you.
Treasure these few words till we're
together
keep all my love forever.
P.S. I love you, you, you, you.
As I write this letter, send my love to you,
(you know I want you to)
remember that I'll always be in love with
you.
I'll be coming home again to you love,
until the day I do love.
P.S. I love you, you, you, you.
I love you.

P.S. I love you
**"I didn't really feel I belonged
until after the first two years,
maybe two and a half. You know,
before it was them, the Beatles
and me–the new drummer.
It lasted long enough to bother me a
bit, but not any more."**–Ringo

"The copper came to the door, to tell
us about the accident. It was just like
it's supposed to be, the way it is in the
films. Asking if I was her son, and all
that. Then he told us, and we both
went white. It was the worst thing that
ever happened to me." –John

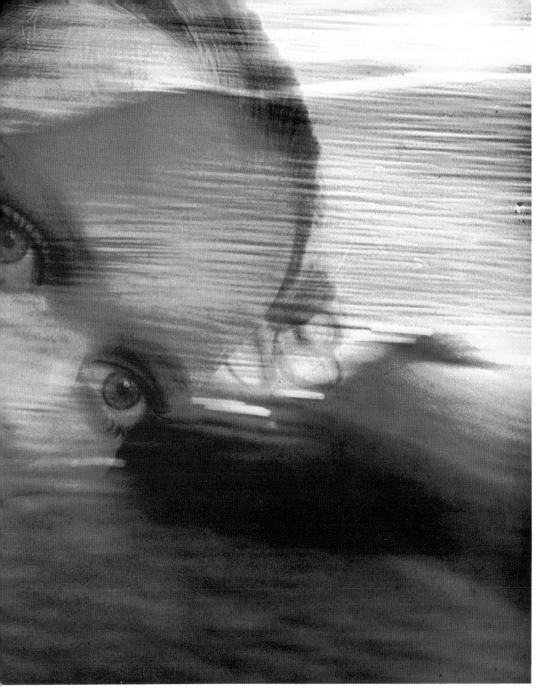

Julia

Half of what I say is meaningless
But I say it just to reach you, Julia.
Julia, Julia, oceanchild, calls me
So I sing a song of love, Julia
Julia, seashell eyes, windy smile, calls me

So I sing a song of love, Julia.
Her hair of floating sky is shimmering, glimmering,
In the sun.
Julia, Julia, morning moon, touch me
So I sing a song of love, Julia.
When I cannot sing my heart

I can only speak my mind, Julia.
Julia, sleeping sand, silent cloud, touch me
So I sing a song of love, Julia.
Hum hum hum hum . . . calls me
So I sing a song of love for Julia, Julia, Julia.

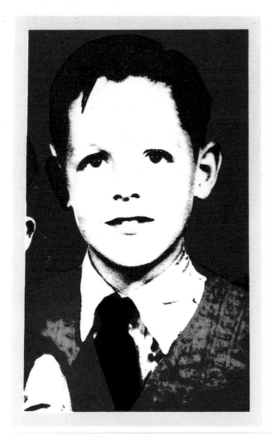

Instant Karma!

Instant Karma's gonna get you, gonna
knock you right on the head,
You better get yourself together pretty
soon, you're gonna be dead,
What in the world were you thinking of
Laughing in the face of love, what on
earth you tryin' to do,
it's up to you, yeah you.
Instant Karma's gonna get you, gonna
look you right in the face,
You better get yourself together darlin'
join the human race.
How in the world you gonna see
Laughin' at fools like me.
Who on earth d'you think you are, a super
star
Well alright you are.
Well we all shine on like the moon and the
stars and the sun.
Well we all shine on ev'ry one come on.
Instant Karma's gonna get you, gonna
knock you off your feet,
Better recognise your brothers ev'ry one
you meet.
Why in the world are we here?
Surely not to live in pain and fear,
Why on earth are you there, when you're
ev'rywhere,
Come and get your share,
Well we all shine on like the moon and the
stars and the sun.
Well we all shine on,
Come on and on and on on
Yeh yeh alright ah ha.

Instant Karma! "I wrote this in the
morning, recorded it that night and
released it the next week. It had to
battle with Let It Be in the American
charts, and it lost. It was a nice
happy-go-lucky song, and has the same
chord sequence as All You Need Is
Love." – John

154

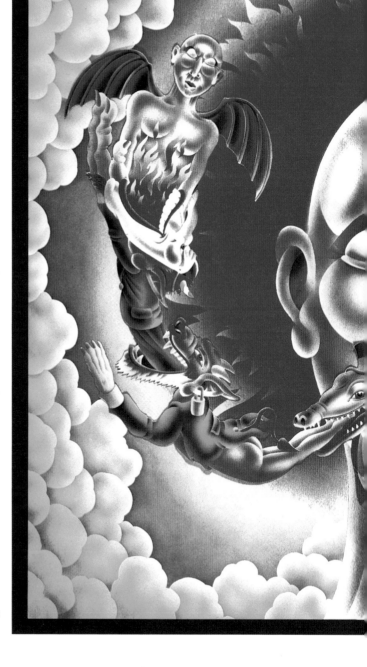

155

I'll be on my way   "The circus has left town but we still own the site." –John

I'll be on my way

The sun is fading away.
That's the end of the day.
As the June-light
turns to moonlight
I'll be on my way.
Just one kiss then I'll go.
Don't hide the tears that don't show.
As the June-light
turns to moonlight
I'll be on my way.
To where the winds don't blow
and golden rivers flow,
this way I will go.
They were right, I was wrong,
true love didn't last long.
As the June-light
turns to moonlight
I'll be on my way.
To where the winds don't blow
and golden rivers flow,
this way I will go.
They were right, I was wrong,
true love didn't last long.
As the June-light
turns to moonlight
I'll be on my way.

I'll cry instead

I've got every reason on earth to be mad,
'cos I've lost the only girl I had.
If I could get my way, I'd get myself
locked up today,
but I can't, so I'll cry instead.
I've got a chip on my shoulder that's
bigger than my feet.
I can't talk to people that I meet.
If I could see you now, I'd try to make you
say it somehow,
but I can't, so I'll cry instead.
Don't want to cry when there's people
there,
I get shy when they start to stare.
I'm gonna hide myself away-ay-hay,
but I'll come back again some day.
And when I do you'd better hide all the
girls,
I'm gonna break their hearts all round the
world,
yes, I'm gonna break them in two and
show you what your lovin' man can do,
until then I'll cry instead.
Don't want to cry when there's people
there,
I get shy when they start to stare.
I'm gonna hide myself away-ay-hay,
but I'll come back again some day.
And when I do you better hide all the girls,
I'm gonna break their hearts all round the
world,
yes, I'm gonna break them in two and
show you what your lovin' man can do,
until then I'll cry instead.

**I'll cry instead "We were going to do
this in *A Hard Day's Night* but the
director Dick Lester didn't like it, so
we put it on the flip side of the album.
I like it."–John**

157

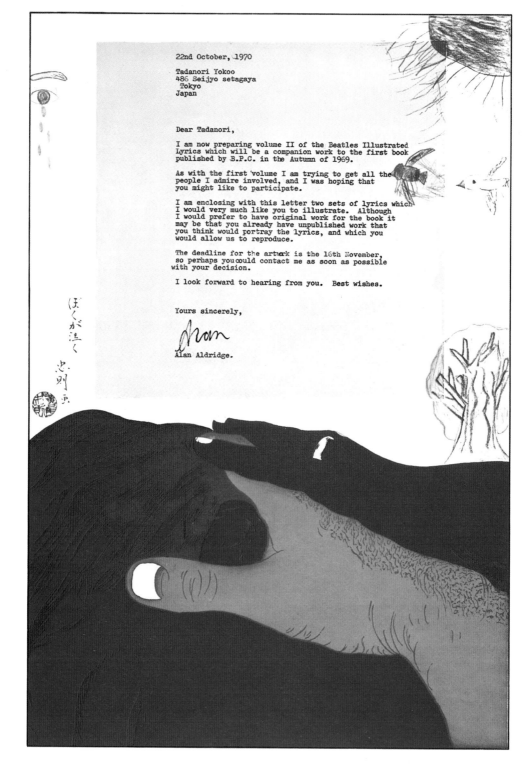

22nd October, 1970

Tadanori Yokoo
486 Seijyo setagaya
Tokyo
Japan

Dear Tadanori,

I am now preparing volume II of the Beatles Illustrated
Lyrics which will be a companion work to the first book
published by B.P.C. in the Autumn of 1969.

As with the first volume I am trying to get all the
people I admire involved, and I was hoping that
you might like to participate.

I am enclosing with this letter two sets of lyrics which
I would very much like you to illustrate. Although
I would prefer to have original work for the book it
may be that you already have unpublished work that
you think would portray the lyrics, and which you
would allow us to reproduce.

The deadline for the artwork is the 16th November,
so perhaps you could contact me as soon as possible
with your decision.

I look forward to hearing from you. Best wishes.

Yours sincerely,

Alan Aldridge.

I'll cry instead

159

When I get home

When I get home

Whoa-ho, whoa-ho,
I got a whole lot of things to tell her, when
I get home,
Come on, I'm on my way,
'cos I'm gonna see my baby today,
I've got a whole lot of things I've gotta say
to her.
Whoa-ho, whoa-ho,
I got a whole lot of things to tell her, when
I get home.
Come on if you please,
I've got no time for trivialities,
I've got a girl who's waiting home for me
tonight.
Whoa-ho, whoa-ho,
I got a whole lot of things to tell her when
I get home.
When I'm getting home tonight, I'm gonna
hold her tight,
I'm gonna love her till the cows come
home,
I bet I'll love her more,
till I walk out that door – again.
Come on, let me through,
I've got so many things, I've got to do,

I've got no business being here with you
this way.
Whoa-ho, whoa-ho,
I've got a whole lot of things to tell her
when I get home – Yeah.

When I get home "There's still
nothing I like more than to get on a
Crosville bus in Liverpool and to go
out for the day somewhere into
Cheshire." – Paul

Woman "It became very difficult for
me to write with Yoko sitting there. I
might want to say something like 'I
love you girl' but with Yoko watching
I always felt I had to come out with
something clever and avant garde. She
would probably have loved the simple
stuff, but I was scared." – Paul

Woman

Woman do you love me?
Woman if you need me then believe me
I need you to be my woman.
Woman do you love me?
Woman if you need me then believe me
I need you to be my woman.
And should you ask me how I'm doing
what shall I say, things are O.K.
Well I know that they're not
and I still may have lost you.
Woman do you love me?
Woman if you need me then believe me
I need you to be my woman.
And should you take your time and tell me
when we're alone, love will come home
I would give up my world
if you'll say that my girl is my woman.
I've got plenty of time,
help me just to get through it.
Once again you'll be mine
I still think we can do it.
And you know how much I love you.
Woman don't forsake me.
Woman if you take me then believe me
I'll take you to be my woman.

It's only love

I get high when I see you go by,
my oh my,
when you sigh, my, my inside just dries,
butterflies,
why am I so shy when I'm beside you?
It's only love and that is all,
why should I feel the way I do?
It's only love and that is all,
but it's so hard loving you.
Is it right that you and I should fight
every night?
Just the sight of you makes night time
bright,
very bright.
Haven't I the right to make it up, girl?
It's only love and that is all,
why should I feel the way I do?
It's only love and that is all,
but it's so hard loving you.
Yes, it's so hard loving you, oh.

Things we said today

You say you will love me if I have to go,
you'll be thinking of me, somehow I will
know,
someday when I'm lonely, wishing you
weren't so far away,
then I will remember things we said today.
You say you will be mine, girl, till the end
of time,
these days such a kind girl seems so hard
to find,
someday when we're dreaming, deep in
love, not a lot to say,
then I will remember things we said today.
Me I'm just a lucky kind,
love to hear you say that love is love,
and though we may be blind,
love is here to stay.
And that's enough to make you mine girl,
be the only one,
love me all the time girl, we'll go on and
on,
someday when we're dreaming, deep in
love, not a lot to say,
then we will remember things we said
today.
Me I'm just a lucky kind,
love to hear you say that love is love
and though we may be blind,
love is here to stay.
And that's enough to make you mine girl,
be the only one,
love me all the time girl, we'll go on and
on,
someday when we're dreaming, deep in
love, not a lot to say,
then we will remember things we said
today.

It's only love "I can't forgive Paul and George for the way they treated Yoko at first, but I can't help loving them either." – John

Things we said today "The nicest thing is to open the newspapers and not to find yourself in them." – George

"We all have Hitler in us, but we also have love and peace. So why not give peace a chance for once?" –John

World without love

Please lock me away,
and don't allow the day
here inside, where I hide with my
loneliness,
I don't care what they say,
I won't stay in a world without love.
Birds sing out of tune,
and rain clouds hide the moon,
I'm O.K., here I'll stay with my loneliness,
I don't care what they say,
I won't stay in a world without love.
So I wait, and in a while
I will see my true love smile,
she may come, I know not when,
when she does I'll know,
so baby, until then—
Lock me away,
and don't allow the day
here inside where I hide with my loneliness,
I don't care what they say,
I won't stay in a world without love.
So I wait, and in a while
I will see my true love smile,
she may come, I know not when,
when she does I'll know,
so baby, until then—
Lock me away,
and don't allow the day
here inside where I hide with my loneliness,
I don't care what they say,
I won't stay in a world without love.
I don't care what they say,
I won't stay in a world without love.

Thank you girl

Oh, oh,
you've been good to me, you made me
glad when I was blue,
and eternally I'll always be in love with
you,
and all I gotta do is thank you girl, thank
you girl.
I could tell the world, a thing or two about
our love,
I know little girl, only a fool would doubt
our love.
and all I gotta do is thank you girl, thank
you girl.
Thank you girl for loving me the way that
you do, (way that you do),
that's the kind of love that is too good to
be true,
and all I gotta do is thank you girl, thank
you girl.
Oh, oh,
you've been good to me, you made me
glad when I was blue,
and all I gotta do is thank you girl, thank
you girl.
Oh, oh.

Thank you girl "Paul and I wrote
this as a B-side for one of our first
records. In the old days we used to
write and write all the time, but
nowadays I only do it if I'm
particularly inspired."–John

Give peace a chance

Two one two three four
Ev'rybody's talking about
Bagism, Shagism, Dragism, Madism,
Ragism, Tagism,
This-ism, That-ism, Is-m, is-m, is-m.
All we are saying is give peace a chance,
All we are saying is give peace a chance
C'mon.
Ev'rybody's talking about Ministers,
Sinisters, Banisters
And canisters, Bishops, and Fishops,
Rabbis and Pop eyes, Bye bye, bye byes.
All we are saying is give peace a chance,
All we are saying is give peace a chance,
Let me tell you now
Revolution, evolution, mastication,
flagellation, regulations, integrations,
meditations, United Nations,
Congratulations.
Oh let's stick to it,
John and Yoko, Timmy Leary, Rosemary,
Tommy Smothers, Bobby Dylan, Tommy
Cooper, Derek Taylor, Norman Mailer,
Alan Ginsberg, Hare Krishna, Hare
Krishna.

Give peace a chance "The real word I
used on the record was
'masturbation', but I'd just got in
trouble for The Ballad of John and
Yoko and I didn't want any more fuss,
so I put 'mastication' in the written
lyrics. It was a cop-out, but the
message about peace was more
important to me than having a little
laugh about a word."–John

Tip of my tongue

When I want to speak to you,
it sometimes takes a week or two
to think of things I want to say to you,
but words just stay on the tip of my
tongue.
When the skies are not so blue,
there's nothing left for me to do
just think of something new to say to you,
but words just stay on the tip of my
tongue.
People say I'm lonely,
only you know that's not true.
You know I'm waiting for a chance
to prove my love to you.
Soon enough my time will come,
and after all is said and done
I'll marry you and we will live as one,
with no more words on the tip of my
tongue no more,
no words on the tip of my tongue.

Tip of my tongue "When I was about
twelve I used to think I must be a
genius, but nobody's noticed. If there is
such a thing as genius I am one,
and if there isn't I don't care."—John

The night before

We said our goodbyes (on the night
before),
love was in your eyes
now today I find, you have changed your
mind,
treat me like you did the night before.
Were you telling lies (on the night before)?
Was I so unwise (on the night before)?
When I held you near, you were so sincere,
treat me like you did the night before.
Last night is the night I will remember you
by,
when I think of things you did it makes me
wanna cry.
We said our goodbyes (on the night
before),
love was in your eyes
now today I find you have changed your
mind,
treat me like you did the night before.
When I held you near, you were so sincere,
treat me like you did the night before.
Last night is the night I will remember you
by,
when I think of things we did it makes me
wanna cry.
Were you telling lies (on the night before)?
Was I so unwise?
When I held you near, you were so sincere,
treat me like you did the night before.

I'll be back

You know if you break my heart, I'll go
but I'll be back again,
'cos I told you once before good-bye, but I
came back again,
I love you so—oh, I'm the one who wants
you oh, oh.
You could find better things to do, than to
break my heart again,
this time I will try to show that I'm not
trying to pretend,
I thought that you would realise,
that if I ran away from you,
that you would want me too,
but I've got a big surprise oh, oh.
Oh, you could find better things to do than
to break my heart again,
this time I will try to show that I'm not
trying to pretend,
I wanna go, but I hate to leave you,
you know, I hate to leave you oh, oh.
Oh, if you break my heart, I'll go,
but I'll be back again.

<u>The night before</u> "How often did we enjoy a show? Once in how many weeks of touring? All that talk about gigs and clubs is a dream—well, more like a nightmare actually. One show in thirty would give us real satisfaction and you'd go through all kinds of hell for that."—John

I'll be back "An early favourite that I wrote." –John

I should have known better "I don't play the sitar now. It would have taken me about ten years to study it, and I have other things which have to be done. The more I've learnt about it the more I've realised how little I know."—George

I should have known better

I should have known better with a girl like you,
that I would love everything that you do,
and I do, hey hey, and I do.
Whoa, whoa, I never realised what a kiss could be,
this could only happen to me,
can't you see, can't you see?
That when I tell you that I love you, oh,
you're gonna say you love me too hoo hoo hoo hoo, oh,
and when I ask you to be mine,
you're gonna say you love me too.
So, oh, I should have realised a lot of things before,
if this is love you've got to give me more,
give me more, hey hey, give me more.
Whoa, whoa, I never realised what a kiss could be,
this could only happen to me,
can't you see, can't you see?
That when I tell you that I love you, oh,
you're gonna say you love me too, oh,
and when I ask you to be mine,
you're gonna say you love me too.
You love me too,
you love me too.

Mean Mr. Mustard

Mean Mister Mustard sleeps in the park,
shaves in the dark
trying to save paper.
Sleeps in a hole in the road
Saving up to buy some clothes.
Keeps a ten bob note up his nose,
Such a mean old man, such a mean old
man.
His sister Pam works in a shop,
She never stops, she's a go getter.
Takes him out to look at the Queen,
Only place that he's ever been.
Always shouts out something obscene,
Such a dirty old man, dirty old man.

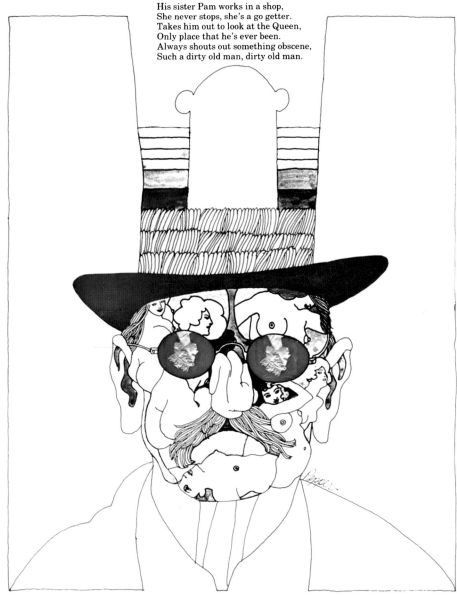

Mean Mr. Mustard "This was just
one of those written in India." —John

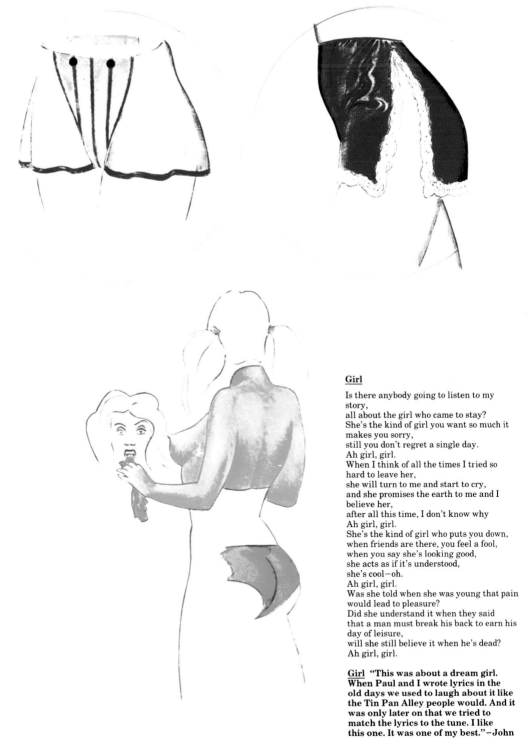

Girl

Is there anybody going to listen to my story,
all about the girl who came to stay?
She's the kind of girl you want so much it makes you sorry,
still you don't regret a single day.
Ah girl, girl.
When I think of all the times I tried so hard to leave her,
she will turn to me and start to cry,
and she promises the earth to me and I believe her,
after all this time, I don't know why
Ah girl, girl.
She's the kind of girl who puts you down,
when friends are there, you feel a fool,
when you say she's looking good,
she acts as if it's understood,
she's cool—oh.
Ah girl, girl.
Was she told when she was young that pain would lead to pleasure?
Did she understand it when they said
that a man must break his back to earn his day of leisure,
will she still believe it when he's dead?
Ah girl, girl.

Girl "This was about a dream girl.
When Paul and I wrote lyrics in the
old days we used to laugh about it like
the Tin Pan Alley people would. And it
was only later on that we tried to
match the lyrics to the tune. I like
this one. It was one of my best."—John

175

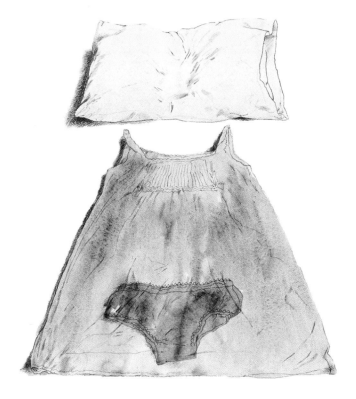

Yes it is

If you wear red tonight,
remember what I said tonight,
for red is the colour my baby wore,
and what's more, it's true,
yes it is.
Scarlet were the clothes she wore,
ev'rybody knows I'm sure,
I would remember all the things we
planned,
understand it's true,
yes, it is true,
yes it is.
I could be happy with you by my side,
if I could forget her,
but it's my pride,
yes it is, yes it is,
Please don't wear red tonight,
this is what I said tonight,
for red is the colour that will make me
blue,
in spite of you it's true,
yes it is it's true,
yes it is.
I could be happy with you by my side,
if I could forget her,
but it's my pride,
yes it is, yes it is.
Please don't wear red tonight,
this is what I said tonight,
for red is the colour that will make me
blue,
in spite of you it's true,
yes it is, it's true.

Yes it is "We're unassuming,
unaffected and British to the core.
Someone asked me once why I wore
rings on my fingers, and when I told
him it was because I couldn't get
them on my nose, he didn't believe
me."–Ringo

Loved of the loved "You can't blame
John for falling in love with Yoko any
more than you can blame me for
falling in love with Linda. At the
beginning I was annoyed with him,
jealous because of Yoko, and afraid
about the break-up of a great musical
partnership. It took me a year to
realise they were in love."–Paul

Love of the loved

Each time I look into your eyes,
I see that there the heaven lies,
and as I look I see the love of the loved.
Someday they'll see that from the start,
my place has been deep in your heart,
and in your heart I see the love of the
loved.
Though I've said it all before, I'll say it
more and more,
now that I'm really sure you love me,
and I know that from today I'll see it in
the way,
that you look at me and say you love me
So let it rain what do I care,
deep in your heart I'll still be there,
and when I'm there I see the love of the
loved.
Though I've said it all before, I'll say it
more and more,
now that I'm really sure you love me,
and I know that from today, I'll see it in
the way,
that you look at me and say you love me.
So let it rain, what do I care,
deep in your heart I'll still be there,
and when I'm there, I see the love of the
loved.
I see the love of the loved.

I'm in love

I've got something to tell you, I'm in love,
I've been longing to tell you, I'm in love.
You'll believe me, when I tell you, I'm in
love with you.
You're my kind of girl
You make me feel proud,
You make me want to shout aloud,
yes, I'm telling all my friends, I'm in love.
Ev'ry night I can't sleep, thinking of you,
and ev'ry little thing that you do,
yes, I'm telling all my friends, I'm in love.
Oh yeh, I'm sittin' on the top of the world,

I'm in love with a wonderful girl,
and I never felt so good before,
if this is love, give me more, more, more.
Ev'ry night I can't sleep, thinking of you,
and ev'ry little thing that you do,
yes, I'm telling all my friends, I'm in love.
Yes, I'm telling all my friends, I'm in love,
in love.
Yes, I'm telling all my friends, I'm in love.

I'm in love "I wrote this for the
Fourmost."—John

Dig a pony

I dig a pony
Well you can celebrate anything you want
Yes you can celebrate anything you want
Ooh.
I do a road hog
Well you can penetrate any place you go,
Yes you can penetrate any place you go
I told you so, all I want is you.
Ev'rything has got to be just like you want
it to.
Because—
I pick a moon dog
Well you can radiate ev'rything you are
Yes you can radiate ev'rything you are—
Ooh.
I roll a stoney
Well you can imitate ev'ryone you know
Yes you can imitate ev'ryone you know.
I told you so, all I want is you.
Ev'rything has got to be just like you want
it to.
Because—
I feel the wind blow
Well you can indicate ev'rything you see
Yes you can indicate ev'rything you see—
Ooh.
I dug a pony
Well you can syndicate any boat you row
Yes you can syndicate any boat you row.
I told you so, all I want is you.
Ev'rything has got to be just like you want
it to.
Because—

Dig a pony "Recording gave us the
advantage of being able to make up
music as we went along."—George
Martin, the Beatles' record producer

All my loving

Close your eyes and I'll kiss you,
tomorrow I'll miss you,
remember I'll always be true,
and then while I'm away,
I'll write home every day,
and I'll send all my loving to you.
I'll pretend I am kissing,
the lips I am missing,
and hope that my dreams will come true,
and then while I'm away,
I'll write home every day,
and I'll send all my loving to you.
All my loving, I will send to you,
all my loving, darling, I'll be true.
Close your eyes and I'll kiss you,
tomorrow I'll miss you,
remember I'll always be true,
and then while I'm away,
I'll write home every day,
and I'll send all my loving to you.
All my loving, I will send to you,
all my loving, darling, I'll be true,
all my loving, I will send to you.

All my loving "I get tired of reading
that I'm some kind of hermit having
an awful time. I'm having a **great**
time. I can see how it all happened. I
was always the ambassador for the
Beatles, but now all I want to do is be
with my family." – Paul

Little child

Little child, little child,
little child, won't you dance with me?
I'm so sad and lonely,
baby take a chance with me.
Little child, little child,
little child, won't you dance with me?
I'm so sad and lonely,
baby take a chance with me.
If you want someone to make you feel so
so fine,
then we'll have some fun when you're
mine, all mine,
so come on, come on, come on.
Little child, little child,
little child, won't you dance with me?
I'm so sad and lonely,
baby take a chance with me.
When you're by my side, you're the only
one,
don't you run and hide, just come on,
come on,
so come on, come on, come on, come on.
Little child, little child,
little child won't you dance with me?
I'm so sad and lonely,
baby take a chance with me.
Oh yeh, baby take a chance with me.

Little child "We had a ward band in
in hospital. There were four kids on
cymbals and two on triangles. I would
never play unless I had a drum." –
Ringo, talking about the year he spent
in hospital as a child of seven

Another girl

For I have got another girl, another girl,
you're making me say that I've got nobody
but you,
but as from today well I've got somebody
that's new,
I ain't no fool and I don't take what I
don't want,
for I have got another girl, another girl.
She's sweeter than all the girls and I've met
quite a few,
nobody in all the world can do what she
can do,
and so I'm telling you this time you'd
better stop,
for I have got another girl.
Another girl, who will love me till the end,
through thick and thin she will always be
my friend.
I don't wanna say that I've been unhappy
with you,
but as from today well I've seen somebody
that's new,
I ain't no fool and I don't take what I
don't want,
for I have got another girl.
Another girl, who will love me till the end,
through thick and thin she will always be
my friend.
I don't wanna say that I've been unhappy
with you,
but as from today well I've seen somebody
that's new,
I ain't no fool and I don't take what I don't
want,
for I have got another girl.

Another girl "I love Yoko. I don't love Cynthia."—John to newspapermen after the break-up of his first marriage.

183

It won't be long

It won't be long yeh, yeh,
it won't be long yeh, yeh,
it won't be long yeh, yeh,
till I belong to you.
Ev'ry night when ev'rybody has fun,
here am I sitting all on my own.
It won't be long yeh, yeh,
it won't be long yeh, yeh,
it won't be long yeh, yeh,
till I belong to you.
Since you left me I'm so alone,
now you're coming, you're coming home,
I'll be good like I know I should,
you're coming home, you're coming home.
Ev'ry night the tears come down from my
eyes,
ev'ry day I've done nothing but cry.
It won't be long yeh, yeh.
Since you left me I'm so alone,
now you're coming, you're coming home,
I'll be good like I know I should,
you're coming home, you're coming home.
Ev'ry day we'll be happy, I know,
now I know that you won't leave me no
more.
It won't be long yeh, yeh.

It won't be long "Another early one.
When I was in therapy in California
they made me go through every lyric
of every song I'd ever written. I
couldn't believe I'd written so many
songs."–John

185

Anytime at all

Anytime at all,
anytime at all,
anytime at all,
all you've gotta do is call,
and I'll be there.
If you need somebody to love,
just look into my eyes,
I'll be there to make you feel right,
if you're feeling sorry and sad, I'd really
sympathise.
Don't be sad, just call me tonight.
Anytime at all,
anytime at all,
anytime at all,
all you gotta do is call,
and I'll be there.
If the sun has faded away,
I'll try to make it shine.
There is nothing I won't do,
if you need a shoulder to cry on, I hope it
will be mine,
call me tonight and I'll come tonight.
Anytime at all,
anytime at all,
anytime at all,
all you've gotta do is call,
and I'll be there.
Anytime at all,
anytime at all,
anytime at all,
all you gotta do is call,
and I'll be there.
Anytime at all,
all you've gotta do is call,
and I'll be there.

Anytime at all "Another of those songs we wrote about the time of 'A Hard Day's Night'. I don't write in the same way anymore, but I suppose I could if I tried."—John

Across the universe

Words are flying out like endless rain into
a paper cup,
They slither while, they pass, they slip
away across the universe.
Pools of sorrow, waves of joy are drifting
through my open mind,
possessing and caressing me.
Jai Guru De Va Om
Nothing's gonna change my world
Nothing's gonna change my world.
Images of broken light which dance before
me like a million eyes,
That call me on and on across the universe,
Thoughts meander like a restless wind
inside a letter box they
tumble blindly as they make their way
across the universe
Jai Guru De Va Om
Nothing's gonna change my world
Nothing's gonna change my world.
Sounds of laughter shades of earth are
ringing through my open
views inciting and inviting me.
Limitless undying love which shines
around me like a million
suns, it calls me on and on across the
universe
Jai Guru De Va Om
Nothing's gonna change my world
Nothing's gonna change my world.

Across the universe "This was one of my favourite songs, but it's been issued in so many forms that it's missed it as a record. I gave it at first to the World Wild Life Fund, but they didn't do much with it, and then we put on the Let It Be album."—John

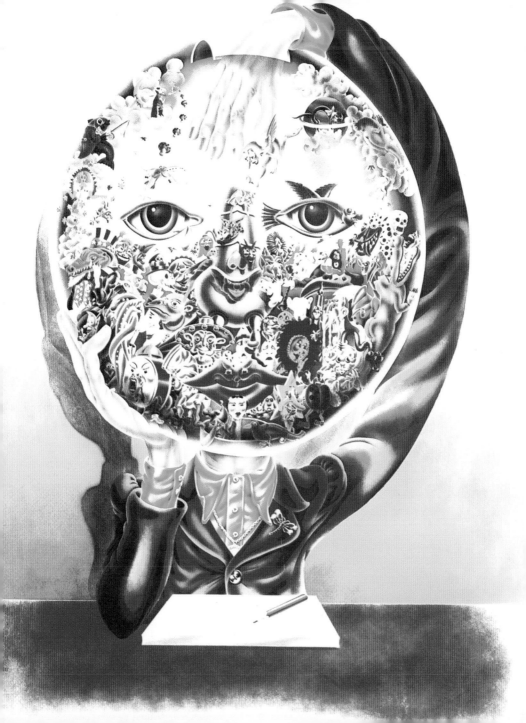

Step inside love

Step inside love, let me find you a place,
where the cares of the day will be carried away
by the smile on your face.
We are together now and forever, come my way.
Step inside love and stay.
Step inside love, step inside love, step inside love.
I want you to stay.
You look tired love, let me turn down the light
come in out of the cold, rest your head on my shoulder
and love me tonight.
I'll always be here if you should need me, night and day.
Step inside love and stay.
Step inside love, step inside love,
I want you to stay.
When you leave me, say you'll see me again,
for I'll know in my heart we will not be apart
and I'll miss you till then.
We'll be together now and forever, come my way.
Step inside love and stay.
Step inside love (I want you to).
Step inside love (I know I do).
I want you to stay.

Step inside love

"So many people used to queue up for Beatle songs but I wouldn't have asked for one because it would have been embarrassing. But Paul said he'd like to write a signature theme for my television series Cilla at the beginning of 1968. He wrote enough for the TV show itself then he gave me the rest of the lyrics for the recording later, and came to all the band calls just to look after the backing." – Cilla Black

I've got a feeling

"Rock and roll is the music that inspired me to play music. There is nothing conceptually better than rock and roll. No group, be it the Beatles, Dylan or the Stones have ever improved on 'Whole lot of Shaking' for my money. Or maybe I'm like our parents: that's my period and I'll dig it and never leave it."
– John

I've got a feeling

I've got a feeling, a feeling deep inside
Oh yeah, Oh yeah.
I've got a feeling, a feeling I can't hide
Oh no, Oh no, Oh no,
Yeah I've got a feeling.
Oh please believe me
I'd hate to miss the train
Oh yeah, Oh yeah.
An if you leave me I won't be late again
Oh no, Oh no, Oh no.
Yeah I've got a feeling yeah.
All these years I've been wandering around,
wondering how come nobody told me
All that I was looking for was somebody who looked like you.
Ev'rybody had a hard year
Ev'rybody had a good time
Ev'rybody had a wet dream,
Ev'rybody saw the sunshine
Oh yeah, Oh yeah, Oh yeah.
Ev'rybody had a good year,
Ev'rybody let their hair down,
Ev'rybody pull their socks up,
Ev'rybody put their foot down.
Oh yeah, Oh yeah, Oh yeah.

I'm down

Barbara Nessim

It's for you

I'm down

You tell lies thinking I can't see,
You can't cry 'cos you're laughing at me,
I'm down (I'm really down),
I'm down (down on the ground)
I'm down (I'm really down).
How can you laugh,
when you know I'm down? (How can you
laugh?).
Man buys ring woman throws it away,
same old thing happens ev'ry day,
I'm down (I'm really down).
I'm down (down on the ground),
I'm down (I'm really down).
How can you laugh
When you know I'm down? (How can you
laugh?).
We're all alone and there's nobody else,
you still moan "Keep your hands to
yourself",
I'm down (I'm really down).
I'm down (down on the ground)
I'm down (I'm really down),
How can you laugh
When you know I'm down? (How can you
laugh?).
Oh yeah.

It's for you

I'd say some day,
I'm bound to give my heart away,
when I do, it's for you.
Love, true love,
seems to be all I'm thinking of,
but it's true, it's for you.
They said that love was a lie,
told me that I should never try to find
somebody who'd be kind, kind to only me.
So I just tell them, they're right, who
wants a fight?
Tell them, I quite agree, nobody'd love me,
then I look at you, and,
love comes, love shows,
I give my heart and no-one knows that I
do,
it's for you,
it's for you.
They said that love was a lie,
told me that I should never try to find
somebody who'd be kind, kind to only me.
So I just tell them, they're right, who
wants a fight?
Tell them I quite agree, nobody'd love me,
then I look at you, and,
love comes, love shows,
I give my heart and no-one knows that I
do,
it's for you,
it's for you.

One after 909

My baby says she's trav'ling on the One
after Nine-O-Nine,
I said move over honey I'm travelling on
that line.
I said move over once, move over twice,
Come on baby don't be cold as ice.
I said I'm trav'ling on the One after
Nine-O-Nine.
I begged her not to go and I begged her on
my bended knees,
You're only fooling around, you're fooling
around with me.
I said move over once, move over twice,
Come on baby don't be cold as ice.
I said I'm trav'ling on the One after
Nine-O-Nine.
I've got my bag,
run to the station.
Railman says you've got the wrong
location.
I've got my bag,
run right home.
Then I find I've got the number wrong,
Well I said I'm trav'ling on the One after
Nine-O-Nine.
I said move over honey I'm travelling on
that line.
I said move over once, mover over twice,
Come on baby don't be cold as ice.
I said we're trav'ling on the One after
Nine-O,
I said we're trav'ling on the One after
Nine-O,
I said we're trav'ling on the One after
Nine-O-Nine.

I'm down "Normally I'm very quiet.
I've always been delicate. I'm not a
tough guy. I've had a facade of being
tough to protect myself from whatever
was going on. But really I'm very
sensitive and weak." – John

It's for you "I'm jealous of the
mirror." – John

One after 909 "One of the first songs
I ever wrote, which we revived for the
film Let It Be." – John

This boy

That boy took my love away,
he'll regret it someday−i−ay,
but this boy wants you back again.
That boy isn't good for you,
tho' he may want you too,
this boy wants you back again.
Oh, and this boy would be happy,
just to love you, but oh my−yi−yi,
that boy won't be happy,
till he's seen you cry−hi−hi.
This boy wouldn't mind the pain,
would always feel the same,
if this boy gets you back again.
This boy. This boy.

This boy "... expressively unusual
for its lugubrious music, but
harmonically it is one of their most
interesting, with its chains of
pandiatonic clusters ..."−William
Mann, music critic of The Times

195

You never give me your money

You never give me your money
You only give me your funny paper
And in the middle of negotiations you
break down
I never give you my number
I only give you my situation
And in the middle of investigation
I break down.
Out of college money spent
See no future pay no rent.
All the money's gone, nowhere to go.
Any Jobber got the sack,
Monday morning turning back.
Yellow lorry slow, nowhere to go.
But oh – that magic feeling nowhere to go.
One sweet dream
Pick up the bags and get in the limousine.
Soon we'll be away from here.
Step on the gas and wipe that tear away,
One sweet dream came true today, came
true today.
One, two, three, four, five, six, seven,
All good children go to heaven.

You never give me your money "I
wrote this when we were going
through all our financial difficulties at
Apple." – Paul

I wanna be your man

I wanna be your lover baby,
I wanna be your man,
I wanna be your lover baby,
I wanna be your man.
Tell me that you love me baby,
like no other can,
love you like no other baby,
like no other can.
I wanna be your man,
I wanna be your man.
Tell me that you love me baby,
tell me you understand,
tell me that you love me baby,
I wanna be your man.
I wanna be your lover baby,
I wanna be your man,
I wanna be your lover baby,
I wanna be your man.
I wanna be your man,
I wanna be your man.
I wanna be your lover baby,
I wanna be your man,
I wanna be your lover baby,
I wanna be your man.
Tell me that you love me baby,
like no other can,
love you like no other baby,
like no other can.
I wanna be your man,
I wanna be your man.

I wanna be your man "I declare that
the Beatles are mutants. Prototypes of
evolutionary agents sent by God,
endowed with a mysterious power to
create a new human species – a young
race of laughing freemen." – Timothy
Leary

KISS ME!

Sun king

Ah—here comes the Sun king.
Ev'rybody's laughing,
Ev'rybody's happy.
Here comes the Sun king.
Quando paramucho mi amore defelice
corazon
Mundo pararazzi mi amore chicka ferdy
parasol
Cuesto obrigado tanta mucho que can eat
it carousel.

Sun king **"The Beatles are personally
not rich to the extent that most
people think they are. Maybe God
didn't make green apples. But the
Beatles <u>companies</u> are worth it.
Individually, though, they just don't
have that much money, and they
should have it."—Allen Klein**

You're going to lose that girl

You're going to lose that girl,
you're going to lose that girl.
If you don't take her out tonight, she's
going to change her mind,
and I will take her out tonight, and I will
treat her kind.
You're going to lose that girl,
you're going to lose that girl.
If you don't treat her right, my friend,
you're going to find her gone,
'cos I will treat her right, and then you'll
be the lonely one.
You're going to lose that girl,
you're going to lose that girl.
I'll make a point of taking her away from
you, yeah,
the way you treat her what else can I do?
You're going to lose that girl,
you're going to lose that girl.
I'll make a point of taking her away from
you, yeah,
the way you treat her what else can I do?
If you don't take her out tonight, she's
going to change her mind,
and I will take her out tonight, and I will
treat her kind.
You're going to lose that girl,
you're going to lose that girl.

You're going to lose that girl **"This
is one of mine. I wasn't too keen on
lyrics in those days. I didn't think
they counted. Dylan used to come out
with his latest acetate and say 'listen
to the words, man'. And I'd say I
don't listen to the words."—John**

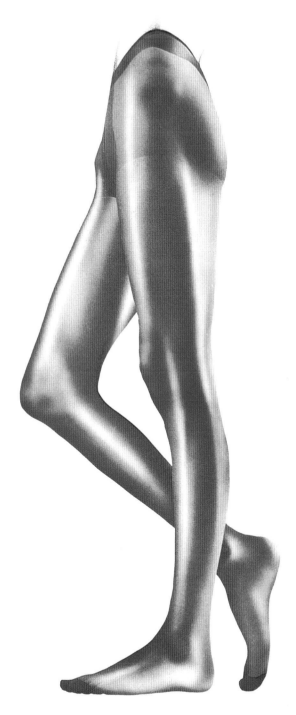

I call your name

I call your name, but you're not there.
Was I to blame for being unfair?
Oh, I can't sleep at night since you've
been gone,
I never weep at night, I can't go on.
Well, don't you know I can't take it?
I don't know who can.
I'm not goin' to make it,
I'm not that kind of man.
Oh, I can't sleep at night, but just the
same,
I never weep at night, I call your name.
Well, don't you know I can't take it?
I don't know who can.
I'm not goin' to make it,
I'm not that kind of man.
Oh, I can't sleep at night, but just the
same,
I never weep at night, I call your name.
I call your name.

I call your name "I like this one. I
wrote it very early on when I was in
Liverpool, and added the middle eight
when we came down to London."
—John

One and one is two

One and one is two,
what am I to do,
now that I'm in love with you.
I'm hoping ev'ry day
I'm gonna hear you say,
you really make my dreams come true.
Can't you feel, when I'm holding you near,
all the things I do
show my love and I'm making it clear,
one and one is two.
One and one is two,
what am I to do
now that I'm in love with you.
I'm hoping ev'ry day
I'm gonna hear you say,
you really make my dreams come true.
Can't you see, I loved you from the start,
don't you love me too?
I love you, but you're breaking my heart
from wanting you.
One and one is two,
what am I to do,
now that I'm in love with you.
I'm hoping ev'ry day,
I'm gonna hear you say

you really make my dreams come true.
If you say that you're gonna be mine,
ev'rything's alright.
All the world would look so fine,
if you'd be mine tonight.
One and one is two,
what am I to do,
now that I'm in love with you.
I'm hoping ev'ry day,
I'm gonna hear you say,
you really make my dreams come true.

One and one is two "I don't know
what John means when he complains
about being short of money. We never
need to carry any with us. If we want
something we sign a piece of paper
and ask them to send the bill to
Apple. He has his car and his house
and anything else he could possibly
want."—Ringo after John had
complained about the Beatles'
financial affairs

201

<u>One and one is two</u>

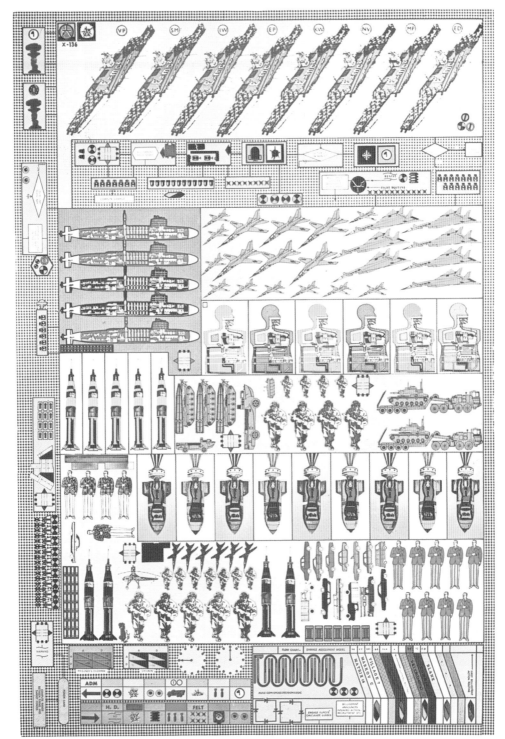

Let it be

Let it be

When I find myself in times of trouble
Mother Mary comes to me
Speaking words of wisdom, let it be.
And in my hour of darkness
She is standing right in front of me
Speaking words of wisdom, let it be.
Let it be, let it be.
Whisper words of wisdom, let it be.
And when the broken hearted people
Living in the world agree,
There will be an answer, let it be.
For though they may be parted there is
Still a chance that they will see
There will be an answer, let it be.
Let it be, let it be. Yeah
There will be an answer, let it be.
And when the night is cloudy,
There is still a light that shines on me,
Shine until tomorrow, let it be.
I wake up to the sound of music,
Mother Mary comes to me,
Speaking words of wisdom, let it be.
Let it be, let it be.
There will be an answer, let it be.
Let it be, let it be,
Whisper words of wisdom, let it be.

Come together

Here come old flat top
He come grooving up slowly
He got joo joo eyeball
He one holy roller
He got hair down to his knee.
Got to be a joker he just do what he please.
He wear no shoe shine
He got toe jam football
He got funny finger
He shoot Coca Cola
He say I know you, you know me.
One thing I can tell you is you got to be free.
Come together right now over me.
Come together.
He bag production
He got walrus gumboot
He got O-no sideboard
He one spinal cracker
He got feet down below his knee.
Hold you in his armchair you can feel his disease.
Come together right now over me.
Come together.
He roller coaster
He got early warning
He got muddy water
He one Mojo filter
He say one and one and one is three.
Got to be goodlooking 'cos he's so hard to see.
Come together right now over me.
Come together.

Let it be "It was hell making the film Let It Be. When it came out a lot of people complained about Yoko looking miserable in it. But even the biggest Beatle fan couldn't have sat through those six weeks of misery. It was the most miserable session on earth."–John

Come together "This is another of my favourites. It was intended as a campaign song at first, but it never turned out that way. People often ask how I write: I do it in all kinds of ways –with piano, guitar, any combination you can think of, in fact. It isn't easy." –John

Tell me why

Tell me why you cried,
and why you lied to me,
tell me why you cried,
and why you lied to me.
Well I gave you ev'rything I had,
but you left me sitting on my own,
did you have to treat me oh so bad,
all I do is hang my head and moan.
Tell me why you cried,
and why you lied to me,
tell me why you cried,
and why you lied to me.
If there's something I have said or done,
tell me what and I'll apologise,
if you don't I really can't go on,
holding back these tears in my eyes.
Tell me why you cried,
and why you lied to me,
tell me why you cried,
and why you lied to me.
Well I beg you on my bended knees,
if you'll only listen to my pleas,
is there anything I can do,
'cos I really can't stand it,
I'm so in love with you.
Tell me why you cried,
and why you lied to me.

Tell me why "You have to be a real
sour square not to love the nutty,
noisy, happy, handsome Beatles." –
Daily Mirror editorial, November 1963

The long and winding road

The long and winding road that leads to
your door,
Will never disappear, I've seen that road
before
It always leads me here, leads me to your
door.
The wild and windy night that the rain
washed away,
Has left a pool of tears crying for the day.
Why leave me standing here, let me know
the way.
Many times I've been alone and many
times I've cried,
Anyway you'll never know the many ways
I've tried, but
Still they lead me back to the long and
winding road,
You left me standing here a long, long time
ago.
Don't leave me waiting here, lead me to
your door.
Da da, da da –

The long and winding road "A few
weeks before this was released Allen
Klein sent me a re-mixed version of it
with harps, horns and orchestra and
women's choir added. No one had
asked me what I thought. I couldn't
believe it. I would <u>never</u> have female
voices on a Beatles record. To me it
was just distasteful." – Paul

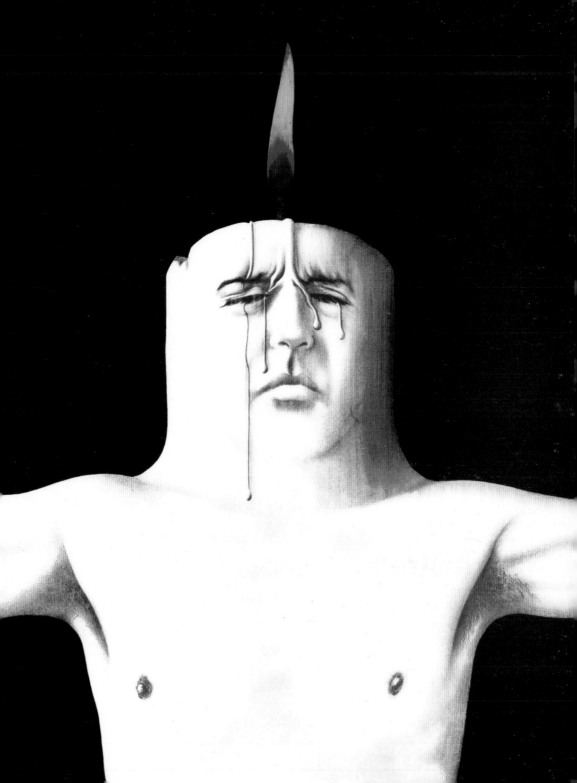

Dig it "I made this up on the spot.

Dig it

Like a Rolling Stone.
A like a Rolling Stone
Like the F.B.I.
and the C.I.A.
And the B.B.C.
B.B. King and Doris Day
Matt Busby.
Dig it. Dig it.

Sounds like it? Yes doesn't it?"—John

208

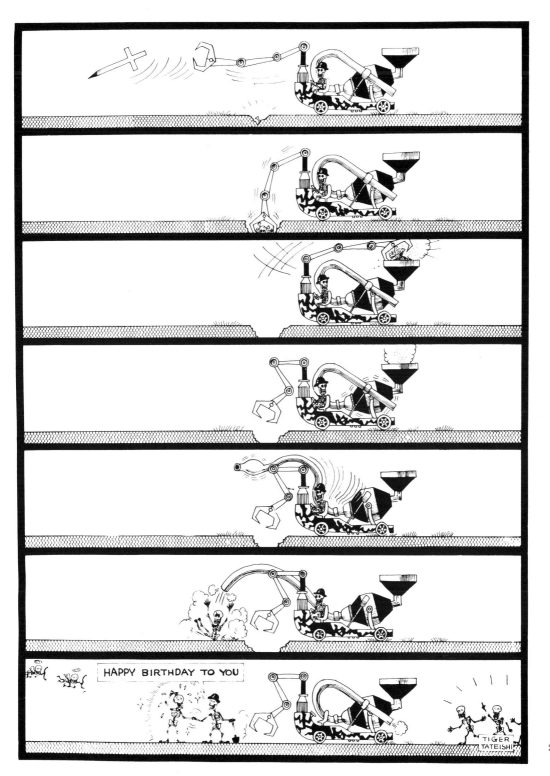

Cold turkey "I wrote this about coming off drugs and the pain involved."–John

She said, she said "I like this one. I wrote it about an acid trip I was on in Los Angeles. It was only the second trip we'd had. We took it because we'd started hearing things about it and we wanted to know what it was all about. Peter Fonda came over to us and started saying things like 'I know what it's like to be dead, man' and we didn't really wanna know, but he kept going on and on. . . . Anyway that's where that song came from and it's a nice song, too."–John

Cold turkey

Temperature's rising
Fever is high
Can't see no future
Can't see no sky.
My feet are so heavy
So is my head
I wish I was a baby
I wish I was dead.
Cold turkey has got me on the run.
Body is aching
Goose-pimple bone
Can't see no body
Leave me alone.
My eyes are wide open
Can't get to sleep
One thing I'm sure of
I'm in at the deep freeze.
Cold turkey has got me on the run.
Cold turkey has got me on the run.
Thirty six hours
Rolling in pain
Praying to someone
Free me again.
Oh I'll be a good boy
Please make me well
I promise you anything
Get me out of this hell.
Cold turkey has got me on the run.

She said she said

She said I know what it's like to be dead,
I know what it is to be sad,
and she's making me feel like I've never been born.
I said who put all those things in your hair,
things that make me feel that I'm mad,
and you're making me feel like I've never been born.
She said you don't understand what I said,
I said no no no you're wrong, when I was a boy,
ev'rything was right, ev'rything was right.
I said even though you know what you know,
I know that I'm ready to leave,
'cos you're making me feel like I've never been born.
She said you don't understand what I said,
I said no no no you're wrong, when I was a boy,
ev'rything was right, ev'rything was right.
I said even though you know what you know,
I know that I'm ready to leave,
'cos you're making me feel like I've never been born.
She said I know what it's like to be dead,
I know what it is to be sad,
I know what it's like to be dead.

210

You can't do that

I got something to say that might cause
you pain,
if I catch you talking to that boy again,
I'm gonna let you down,
and leave you flat,
because I told you before, oh,
you can't do that.
Well, it's the second time I've caught you
talking to him,
do I have to tell you one more time, I
think it's a sin,
I think I'll let you down.
Let you down and leave you flat,
because I've told you before, oh,
you can't do that.
Ev'rybody's green,
'cause I'm the one, who won your love,
but if it's seen,
you're talking that way
they'd laugh in my face.
So please listen to me, if you wanna stay
mine,
I can't help my feelings, I'll go out of my
mind,
I know I'll let you down,

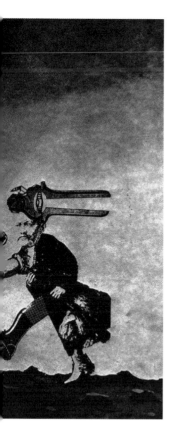

and leave you flat,
gonna let you down and leave you flat,
because I've told you before, oh,
you can't do that.
Ev'rybody's green,
'cause I'm the one who won your love,
but if it's seen,
you're talking that way,
they'd laugh in my face.
So please listen to me, if you wanna stay mine,
I can't help my feelings, I'll go out of my mind,
I know I'll let you down,
and leave you flat,
gonna let you down and leave you flat,
because I've told you before, oh,
you can't do that.
You can't do that.

You can't do that "This was my attempt at being Wilson Pickett at the time, but it was on the flip side because Can't Buy Me Love was so good"–John

Hello little girl

When I see you ev'ry day, I say mm-mm,
hello little girl,
when you're passing on your way, I say
mm-mm, hello little girl.
If I see you passing by, I cry mm-mm,
hello little girl,
when I try to catch your eye, I cry
mm-mm, hello little girl.
I send you flowers, but you don't care,
you never seem to see me standing there.
I often wonder, what you're thinking of,
I hope it's me (love, love, love).
So I hope there'll come a day, when you'll
say mm-mm,
you're my little girl.
When I see you ev'ry day, I say mm-mm,
hello little girl,
when you're passing on your way, I say
mm-mm, hello little girl.
If I see you passing by, I cry mm-mm,
hello little girl,
when I try to catch your eye, I cry
mm-mm, hello little girl.
It's not the first time it's happened to me,
it's been a long, long time and it's so funny
to see
that I'm about to lose my mind.
So I hope there'll come a day, when you'll
say mm-mm, you're my little girl.
You're my little girl.

Hello little girl "This was one of the
first songs I ever finished. I was then
about eighteen and we gave it to the
Fourmost. I think it was the first song
of my own that I ever attempted to do
with the group."–John

She's a woman

My love don't give me presents.
I know that she's no peasant,
only ever has to give love forever and
forever,
my love don't give me presents,
turn me on when I get lonely,
people tell me that she's only foolin',
I know she isn't.
She don't give the boys the eye,
she hates to see me cry,
she is happy just to hear me say that I
will never leave her.
She don't give the boys the eye,
she will never make me jealous,
gives me all her time as well as lovin',
don't ask me why.
She's a woman who understands.
She's a woman who loves her man.
My love don't give me presents.
I know that she's no peasant,
only ever has to give me love forever and
forever,
my love don't give me presents,
turn me on when I get lonely,
people tell me that she's only foolin',
I know she isn't.

She's a woman who understands.
She's a woman who loves her man.
My love don't give me presents.
I know that she's no peasant.
only ever has to give me love forever and
forever,
my love don't give me presents,
turn me on when I get lonely,
people tell me that she's only foolin',
I know she isn't.
She's a woman, she's a woman.

She's a woman Yoko: "I think I'll
go and change." John: "Oh good. I'll
come and watch."

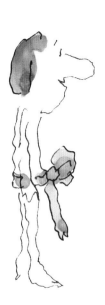

She came in through the bathroom window

Oh look out
She came in through the bathroom
window,
Protected by a silver spoon
But now she sucks her thumb and wonders
by the banks of her own lagoon
Didn't anybody tell her
Didn't anybody see
Sundays on the phone to Monday
Tuesdays on the phone to me.
She said she'd always been a dancer
She worked at fifteen clubs a day
And though she thought I knew the answer
Well I knew what I could not say.
And so I quit the police department
And got myself a steady job
And though she tried her best to help me
She could steal but she could not rob.

She came in through the bathroom window "This forms part of a medley of songs which is about 15 minutes long on 'Abbey Road'. We did it this way because both John and I had a number of songs which were great as they were but which we'd never finished." – Paul

Her Majesty

Her Majesty's a pretty nice girl but she
doesn't have a lot to say.
Her Majesty's a pretty nice girl but she
changes from day to day.
I wanna tell her that I love her a lot,
but I gotta get a belly full of wine.
Her Majesty's a pretty nice girl,
Someday I'm gonna make her mine – Oh
yeah,
Someday I'm gonna make her mine.

Her Majesty "My only regret about the M.B.E. was in ever taking it. It was a sell-out. We would never have got it anyway if the Palace had read what I thought about royalty." – John

216

The ballad of John and Yoko

Standing in the dock at Southampton,
Trying to get to Holland or France.
The man in the mac said you've got to go back,
You know they didn't even give us a chance.
Christ! You know it ain't easy,
You know how hard it can be.
The way things are going,
They're going to crucify me.
Finally made the plane into Paris,
Honeymooning down by the Seine.
Peter Brown called to say,
You can make it O.K.,
You can get married in Gibraltar near Spain.
Christ! You know it ain't easy.
You know how hard it can be.
The way things are going,
They're going to crucify me.
Drove from Paris to the Amsterdam Hilton,
Talking in our beds for a week.
The newspapers said, say what're you doing in bed,
I said we're only trying to get us some peace.
Christ! You know it ain't easy,

You know how hard it can be.
The way things are going,
They're going to crucify me.
Saving up your money for a rainy day,
Giving all your clothes to charity.
Last night the wife said,
Oh boy, when you're dead you don't take nothing with you but your soul—
Think!
Made a lightning trip to Vienna,
Eating choc'late cake in a bag.
The newspapers said,
She's gone to his head,
They look just like two Gurus in drag.
Christ! You know it ain't easy,
You know how hard it can be.
The way things are going,
They're going to crucify me.
Caught the early plane back to London,
Fifty acorns tied in a sack.
The men from the press said we wish you success,
It's good to have the both of you back.
Christ! You know it ain't easy,
You know how hard it can be.
The way things are going,
They're going to crucify me.

Wild honey pie "This was just a fragment of an instrumental which we weren't sure about, but Patti liked it very much so we decided to leave it on the album."—Paul

The ballad of John and Yoko "How can I be lonely when I'm with Yoko day and night? I'm lonely in the universal sense, but there are no outside desires. We are the best things we can give each other."—John

Wild honey pie

Honey pie
Honey pie
Honey pie
Honey pie
Honey pie hello . . . .

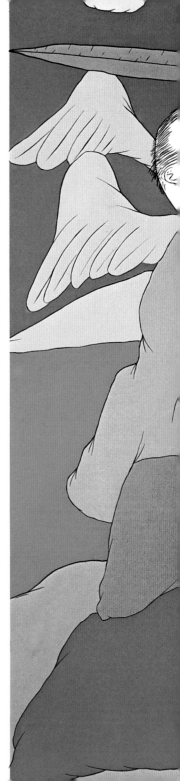

Do you want to know a secret?

You'll never know how much I really love
you,
you'll never know how much I really care.
Listen, do you want to know a secret,
do you promise not to tell?
Who-a, closer, let me whisper in your ear,
say the words I love to hear,
I'm in love with you—oh.
Listen, do you want to know a secret,
do you promise not to tell?
Who-a, closer, let me whisper in your ear,
say the words I love to hear,
I'm in love with you—oh.
I've known the secret for a week or two,
nobody knows, just we two.
Listen, do you want to know a secret,
do you promise not to tell?
Who-a, closer, let me whisper in your ear,
say the words I love to hear,
I'm in love with you—oh.

**Do you want to know a secret? "I
wrote this one. I remember getting
the idea from a Walt Disney film—
Cinderella or Fantasia. It went
something like: 'D'you wanna know a
secret, promise not to tell, standing
by a wishing well' "—John**

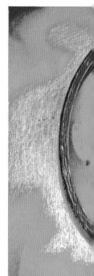

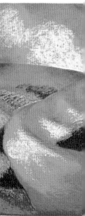

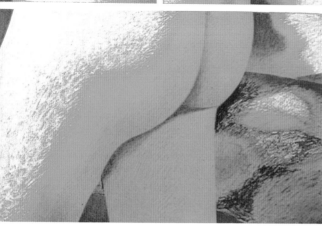

Every little thing

When I'm walking behind her,
people tell me I'm lucky,
yes I know I'm a lucky guy,
I remember the first time
I was lonely without her,
yes, I'm thinking about her now.
Ev'ry little thing she does,
she does for me, yeh,
and you know the things she does,
she does for me, oh.
When I'm with her I'm happy,
just to know that she loves me,
yes I know that she loves me now.
There is one thing I am sure of,
I will love her forever,
for I know love will never die.
Ev'ry little thing she does,
she does for me, yeh,
and you know the things she does,
she does for me, oh.
Ev'ry little thing she does,
she does for me, yeh,
and you know the things she does,
she does for me, oh.

Every little thing "During
Beatlemania Mal Evans and Neil
Aspinall used to sign our autographs
for us. It was Neil who signed the
pictures that were sent to Prince
Charles."—John

What you're doing

Look what you're doing, I'm feeling blue
and lonely,
would it be too much to ask of you, what
you're doing to me?
You got me running and there's no fun
in it,
why should it be so much to ask of you
what you're doing to me?
I've been waiting here for you,
wond'ring what you're gonna do,
should you need a love that's true, it's me.
Please stop your lying, you've got me
crying, girl,
why should it be so much to ask of you,
what you're doing to me?
I've been waiting here for you,
wond'ring what you're gonna do,
should you need a love that's true, it's me.
Please stop your lying, you've got me
crying, girl,
why should it be so much to ask of you,
what you're doing to me?
What you're doing to me.

What you're doing "Henry Ford
knew how to sell cars by advertising.
I'm selling peace, and Yoko and I are
just one big advertising campaign. It
may make people laugh but it may
make them think, too. Really we're
Mr. and Mrs. Peace."—John

Wait

It's been a long time, now I'm coming back home,
I've been away now, oh how I've been alone,
wait till I come back to your side,
we'll forget the tears we cried.
But if your heart breaks, don't wait, turn me away,
and if your heart's strong, hold on, I won't delay,
wait till I come back to your side,
we'll forget the tears we cried.
I feel as though you ought to know
that I've been good, as good as I can be,

and if you do, I'll trust in you,
and know that you will wait for me.
It's been a long time, now I'm coming back home,
I've been away now, oh how I've been alone,
wait till I come back to your side,
we'll forget the tears we cried.
I feel as though you ought to know
that I've been good, as good as I can be,
and if you do, I'll trust in you,
and know that you will wait for me.
But if your heart breaks, don't wait, turn me away,
and if your heart's strong, hold on, I won't delay,

wait till I come back to your side,
we'll forget the tears we cried.
It's been a long time, now I'm coming back home,
I've been away now, oh how I've been alone.

Wait "Lennon and McCartney's lyrics represent an important barometer in our society—sentiments which are shared by pupils in every classroom in Britain."—Times Educational Supplement

Come and get it

If you want it, here it is,
Come and get it
Make your mind up fast.
If you want it any time
I can give it
But you better hurry 'cos it may not last.
Did I hear you say that there must be a
catch
Will you walk away from a fool and his
money?
If you want it, here it is,
Come and get it
But you better hurry 'cos it's going fast.
Sonny if you want it, here it is,
Come and get it,
But you better hurry 'cos it's going fast.
You'd better hurry 'cos it's going fast—
Do—.

Come and get it "Paul told me he'd
written a song for 'The Magic
Christian' film and that Badfinger
could record it if they'd do exactly as
he wanted."—Bill Collins, Manager of
Badfinger

Eight days a week

Ooh I need your love babe, guess you know
it's true,
hope you need my love babe, just like I
need you,
hold me, love me,
hold me, love me,
ain't got nothin' but love babe,
eight days a week.
Love you ev'ry day girl, always on my
mind,
one thing I can say girl, love you all the
time,
hold me, love me,
hold me, love me,
ain't got nothin' but love girl,
eight days a week.
Eight days a week I love you,
eight days a week is not enough to show I
care.
Ooh, I need your love babe guess you
know it's true,
hope you need my love babe, just like I
need you,
hold me, love me,
hold me, love me,
ain't got nothin' but love babe,
eight days a week.
Eight days a week I love you,
eight days a week is not enough to show I
care.
Love you ev'ry day girl, always on my
mind,
one thing I can say girl, love you all the
time,
hold me, love me,
hold me, love me,
ain't got nothin' but love girl,
eight days a week.
Eight days a week. Eight days a week.

Eight days a week "All we want to be
are four rock and rollers, but we aren't
allowed because of Apple. We have to
become businessmen."—Ringo

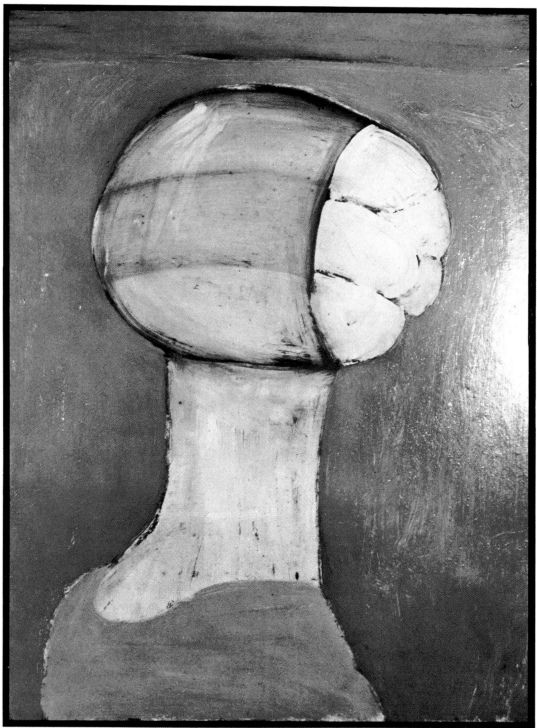

Two of us "I've got a great wife whom I love more today than on the day I married her, two great kids and a nice house. These are precious moments for me." – Paul

Two of us

Two of us riding nowhere
Spending someone's hard earned pay.
You and me Sunday driving,
Not arriving on our way back home.
We're on our way home,
We're on our way home,
We're going home.
You and I have memories
Longer than the road that stretches out ahead.
Two of us sending postcards
Writing letters on my wall.
You and me burning matches,
Lifting latches on our way back home.
We're on our way home,
We're on our way home,
We're going home.
Two of us wearing raincoats
Standing solo in the sun.
You and me chasing paper,
Getting nowhere on our way back home.
We're on our way home,
We're on our way home,
We're going home.

And I love her

I give her all my love,
that's all I do,
and if you saw my love,
you'd love her too.
I love her.
She gives me ev'rything,
and tenderly,
the kiss my lover brings,
she brings to me,
and I love her.
A love like ours,
could never die,
as long as I,
have you near me.
Bright are the stars that shine,
dark is the sky,
I know this love of mine,
will never die,
and I love her.
Bright are the stars that shine,
dark is the sky,
I know this love of mine,
will never die,
and I love her.

<u>And I love her</u> **"When we started
filming I could feel George looking at
me and I was a bit embarrassed. Then
when he was giving me his autograph
he put seven kisses under his name. I
thought he must like me a little."**
−Patti Harrison talking about how
she met George during the filming of
A Hard Day's Night.

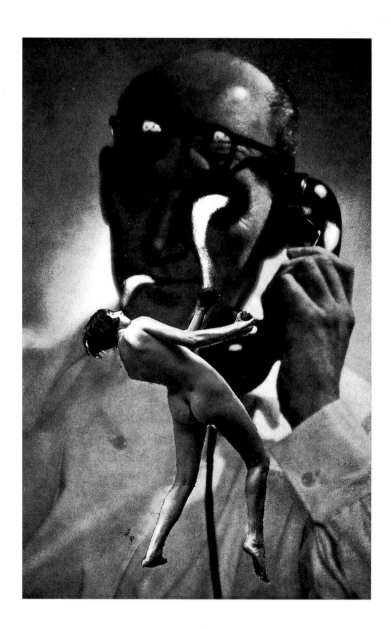

Polythene Pam

Well you should see Polythene Pam
She's so goodlooking but she looks like a
man.
Well you should see her in drag,
Dressed in her polythene bag.
Yes you should see Polythene Pam—Yeh.

Get a dose of her in jackboots and kilt
She's killer diller when she's dressed to the
hilt.
She's the kind of a girl that makes the
News of the World.
Yes you could say she was attractively
built—Yeh.

Polythene Pam "I wrote this one in
India, and when I recorded it I used a
thick Liverpool accent because it was
supposed to be about a mythical
Liverpool scrubber dressed up in her
jackboots and kilt."—John

I don't want to spoil the party

I don't want to spoil the party so I'll go,
I would hate my disappointment to show,
there's nothing for me here so I will disappear,
if she turns up while I'm gone please let me know.
I've had a drink or two and I don't care,
there's no fun in what I do if she's not there,
I wonder what went wrong I've waited far too long,
I think I'll take a walk and look for her.
Though tonight she's made me sad,
I still love her.
If I find her I'll be glad,
I still love her.
I don't want to spoil the party so I'll go,
I would hate my disappointment to show,
there's nothing for me here so I will disappear,
if she turns up while I'm gone please let me know.
Though tonight she's made me sad,
I still love her.

If I find her I'll be glad,
I still love her.
I've had a drink or two and I don't care,
there's no fun in what I do if she's not there,
I wonder what went wrong I've waited far too long,
I think I'll take a walk and look for her.

I don't want to spoil the party "That was a very personal one of mine. In the early days I wrote less material than Paul because he was more competent on guitar than I. He taught me quite a lot of guitar really." – John

Like dreamers do

Dreams, I saw a girl in my dreams.
And so it seems
that I will love her.
You, you are that girl in my dreams.
And so it seems
that I will love her.
And I yi, yi, waited for your kiss,
waited for the bliss.
Like dreamers do.
You, you came just one dream ago.
And now I know
that I will love you.
I knew, when you first said hello.
That's how I know
that I will love you.
And I yi, yi,
oh, I'll be there, yeh,
waiting for you, you.

Like dreamers do "As I see it now we all have a great opportunity for a fantastically lucky life. We don't have to have schedules. We're the way everybody could be if they could afford it." – Paul

235

I don't want to see you again

I don't want to see you again.
I hear that love is planned,
how can I understand,
when someone says to me,
"I don't want to see you again"?
Why do I cry at night?
Something wrong could be right.
I hear you say to me,
"I don't want to see you again."
As you turned your back on me,
you hid the light of day.
I didn't have to play,
at being broken hearted.
I know that later on,
after love's been and gone,
I'd still hear someone say,
"I don't want to see you again."
As you turned your back on me,
you hid the light of day.
I didn't have to play,
at being broken hearted.
I hear that love is planned,
how can I understand,
when someone says to me,
"I don't want to see you again"?
I don't want to see you again.

I want you

I want you
I want you so bad
I want you,
I want you so bad
It's driving me mad, it's driving me mad.
I want you
I want you so bad babe
I want you,
I want you so bad
It's driving me mad, it's driving me mad.
Yeah.
I want you
I want you so bad babe
I want you,
I want you so bad
It's driving me mad, it's driving me mad
I want you
I want you so bad
I want you,
I want you so bad
it's driving me mad, it's driving me mad
Yeah
She's so heavy heavy.

I don't want to see you again "When
I first went out with Ritchie I had to be
careful because of the fans. I might
easily have been killed otherwise. Not
being married was all part of their
image, and none of them were
supposed to have steadies. I always
liked Ritchie the best, although I
remember it was Paul that I kissed
first for a dare."—Maureen Starkey

I want you "This is about Yoko.
She's very heavy, and there was
nothing else I could say about her
other than I want you, she's so heavy.
Someone said the lyrics weren't very
good. But there was nothing more I
wanted to say."—John

MAP XII.

THE SKY.

Nov. 22, at 10 o'clock.	Dec. 3, at 9¼ o'clock.	Dec. 14, at 8½ o'clock.
Nov. 25, at 9¾ o'clock.	Dec. 7, at 9 o'clock.	Dec. 17, at 8¼ o'clock.
Nov. 29, at 9½ o'clock.	Dec. 10, at 8¾ o'clock.	Dec. 21, at 8 o'clock.

IN THE EVENING.

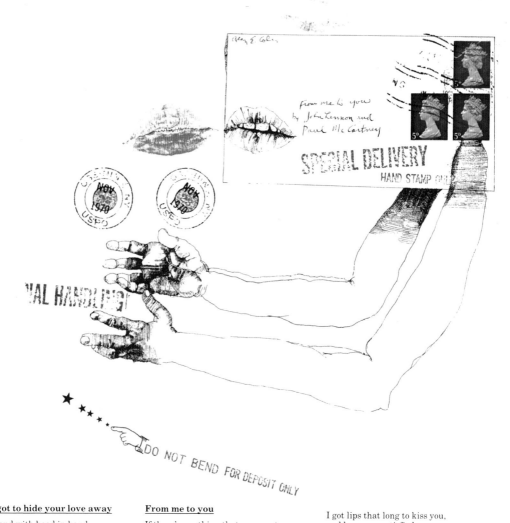

You've got to hide your love away

Here I stand with head in hand,
turn my face to the wall.
If she's gone I can't go on,
feeling two foot small.
Ev'rywhere people stare,
each and ev'ry day.
I can see them laugh at me,
and I hear them say.
Hey, you've got to hide your love away.
Hey, you've got to hide your love away.
How can I even try,
I can never win,
hearing them, seeing them,
in the state I'm in.
How could she say to me
love will find a way?
Gather round all you clowns
let me hear you say.
Hey, you've got to hide your love away.
Hey, you've got to hide your love away.

From me to you

If there's anything that you want,
if there's anything I can do,
just call on me and I'll send it along,
with love from me to you.
I've got ev'rything that you want,
like a heart that's oh so true,
just call on me and I'll send it along,
with love from me to you.
I got arms that long to hold you,
and keep you by my side,
I got lips that long to kiss you,
and keep you satisfied.
If there's anything that you want,
if there's anything I can do,
just call on me and I'll send it along,
with love from me to you.
Just call on me and I'll send it along,
with love from me to you.
I got arms that long to hold you,
and keep you by my side,

I got lips that long to kiss you,
and keep you satisfied.
If there's anything that you want,
if there's anything I can do,
just call on me and I'll send it along,
with love from me to you.

From me to you "Paul and I wrote
this when we were on tour. We nearly
didn't record it because we thought it
was too bluesy at first, but when we'd
finished it and George Martin had
scored it with harmonica it was all
right."—John

You've got to hide your love away
"This was written in my Dylan days
for the film Help. When I was a
teenager I used to write poetry, but
was always trying to hide my real
feelings."—John

239

That means a lot

A friend says that your love won't mean
a lot.
And you know that your love is all you
got.
At times they go so fine
and at times they're not.
But when she says, she loves you,
that means a lot.
A friend says that a love is never true.
And you know that this could apply to
you.
A church can mean so much,
when it's all you got.
But when she says, she loves you,
that means a lot.

Love can be deep inside,
love can be suicide.
Can't you see, you can't hide
what you feel when it's real.
When she says she loves you,
that means a lot.
Can't you see?

x

241

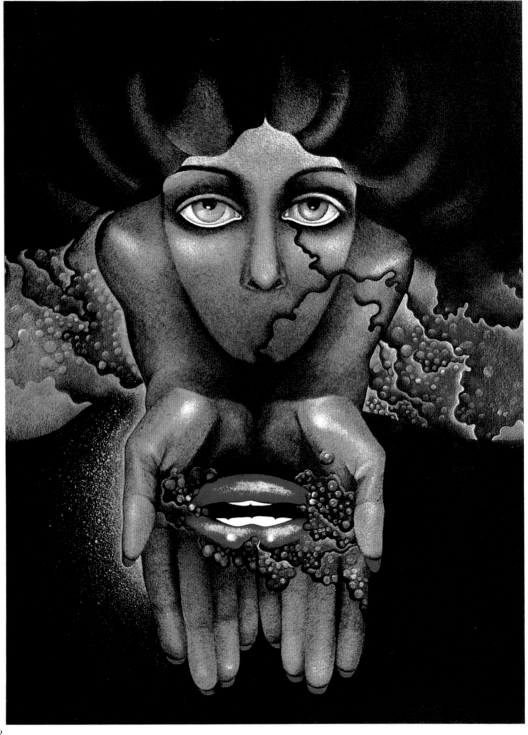

I've just seen a face

I've just seen a face I can't forget the time
or place where we met,
she's just the girl for me and I want the
world to see we've met.
mm mm
Had it been another day I might have
looked the other way and,
I'd have never been aware but as it is I'll
dream of her tonight.
da da
Falling, yes I'm falling,
and she keeps calling me back again.
I have never known the like of this I've
been alone and I have,
missed things and kept out of sight for
other girls were never quite like this.
da da
Falling, yes I am falling,
and she keeps calling me back again.
mm mm
I've just seen a face I can't forget the time
or place where we met,
she's just the girl for me and I want the
world to see we've met.
mm mm
Falling, yes I am falling,
and she keeps calling me back again.

I've just seen a face "I'd like to be
rich and famous but invisible—to be
able to get all the credit and all the
fun, but so that when we went outside
no one would know us."—John

I'll keep you satisfied

You don't need anybody to hold you,
here I stand with my arms open wide,
give me love and remember, what I told
you,
I'll keep you satisfied.
You don't need anybody to kiss you, ev'ry
day I'll be here by your side,
don't go 'way, I'm afraid that I might miss
you,
I'll keep you satisfied.
You can always get a simple thing like
love anytime,
but it's diff'rent with a boy like me and a
love like mine.
So believe ev'rything that I told you,
and agree that with me by your side,
you don't need anybody to hold you,
I'll keep you satisfied.
You can always get a simple thing like
love anytime,
but it's diff'rent with a boy like me and a
love like mine.
So believe ev'rything that I told you,
and agree that with me by your side,
you don't need anybody to hold you.
I'll keep you satisfied.
Give me love and remember, what I told
you,
I'll keep you satisfied.

I'll keep you satisfied "A poached egg
in the Underground on the Bakerloo
line between Trafalgar Square and
Charing Cross? Yes, Paul. A sock full
of elephant's dung on Otterspool
Promenade? Give me ten minutes,
Ringo. Two Turkish dwarfs dancing
the Charleston on the sideboard.
Male or female, John? Hair from Sonny
Liston? It's early closing, George (gulp),
but give me until noon
tomorrow."—Derek Taylor, a former
Beatle aide and Press Officer, talking
about the difficulties of working for
them.

No reply

This happened once before,
when I came to your door, no reply.
They said it wasn't you,
but I saw you peep through your window,
I saw the light, I saw the light,
I know that you saw me,
'cos I looked up to see your face.
I tried to telephone,
they said you were not home, that's a lie,
'cos I know where you've been,
I saw you walk in your door,
I nearly died, I nearly died,
'cos you walked hand in hand
with another man in my place.
If I were you I'd realise that I
love you more than any other guy,
and I'll forgive the lies that I
heard before when you gave me no reply.
I've tried to telephone,
they said you were not home, that's a lie,
'cos I know where you've been,
I saw you walk in your door,
I nearly died, I nearly died,
'cos you walked hand in hand
with another man in my place.
No reply, no reply.

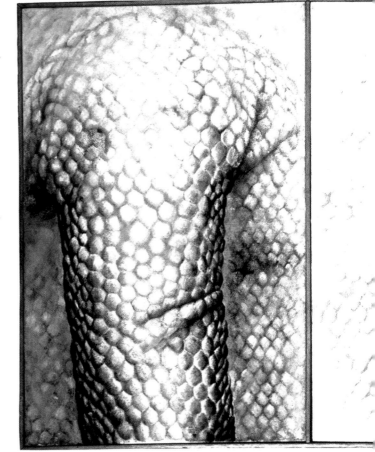

No reply "The greatest composers
since Beethoven." – Richard Buckle
writing in the Sunday Times in
December 1963

244

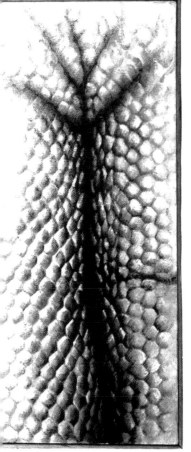

Not a second time

You know you made me cry,
I see no use in wond'ring why,
I cried for you.
And now, you've changed your mind,
I see no reason to change mine,
I cried, it's through, oh.
Oh, you're giving me the same old line,
I'm wond'ring why,
you hurt me then, you're back again,
no, no, not a second time.
You know you made me cry,
I see no use in wond'ring why,
I cried for you, yeh.
And now you've changed your mind,
I see no reason to change mine,
I cried, it's through, oh.
Oh, you're giving me the same old line,
I'm wond'ring why,
you hurt me then, you're back again,
no, no, not a second time.

Not a second time "I wrote this for
the second album, and it was the one
that William Mann wrote about in
The Times. He went on about the flat
sub-mediant key switches and the
Aeolian cadence at the end being like
Mahler's Song of the Earth. Really it
was just chords like any other chords.
That was the first time anyone had
written anything like that about us."
—John

Maxwell's silver hammer

Joan was quizzical studied pataphysical
science in the home
Late night all alone with a test-tube,
oh oh, oh oh.
Maxwell Edison majoring in medicine calls
her on the phone,
Can I take you out to the pictures Joan.
But as she's getting ready to go, a knock
comes on the door.
Bang bang Maxwell's silver hammer came
down upon her head,
Bang bang Maxwell's silver hammer made
sure that she was dead.
Back in school again, Maxwell plays the
fool again, teacher gets annoyed,
Wishing to avoid an unpleasant scene,
She tells Max to stay when the class has
gone away,
So he waits behind,
Writing fifty times I must not be so
But when she turns her back on the boy,
he creeps up from behind,
Bang bang Maxwell's silver hammer came
down upon her head
Bang bang Maxwell's silver hammer made
sure that she was dead.
P.C. thirty-one said, we've caught a dirty
one,
Maxwell stands alone
Painting testimonial pictures oh oh oh oh.
Rose and Valerie screaming from the
gallery say he must go free.
The judge does not agree and he tells them
so oh oh.
But as the words are leaving his lips, a
noise comes from behind,
Bang bang Maxwell's silver hammer came
down upon his head,
Bang bang Maxwell's silver hammer made
sure that he was dead.
Silver hammer man.

I feel fine

Baby's good to me, you know,
she's happy as can be, you know,
she said so.
I'm in love with her and I feel fine.
Baby says she's mine you know,
she tells me all the time you know,
she said so.
I'm in love with her and I feel fine.
I'm so glad that she's my little girl,
she's so glad she's telling all the world.
That her baby buys her things you know,
he buys her diamond rings you know,
she said so.
She's in love with me and I feel fine.
Baby says she's mine you know,
she tells me all the time you know,
she said so.
I'm in love with her and I feel fine.
I'm so glad that she's my little girl,
she's so glad she's telling all the world.
That her baby buys her things you know,
he buys her diamond rings you know,
she said so.
She's in love with me and I feel fine.

Maxwell's silver hammer
"This epitomises the downfalls in life. Just when everything is going smoothly,
'bang bang' down comes Maxwell's silver hammer and ruins everything." – Paul

I feel fine "I wrote this at a recording
session. It was tied together around the
guitar riff that opens it." – John

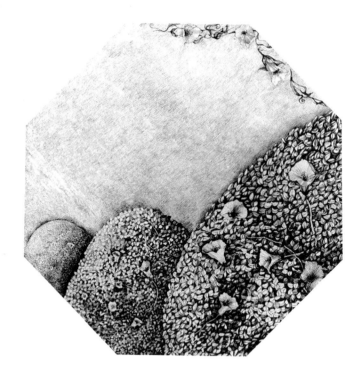

For no one

Your day breaks, your mind aches,
you find that all her words of kindness
linger on,
when she no longer needs you.
She wakes up, she makes up, she takes her
time and doesn't feel she has to hurry,
she no longer needs you.
And in her eyes you see nothing,
no sign of love behind the tears cried for no
one,
a love that should have lasted years.
You want her, you need her,
and yet you don't believe her,
when she says her love is dead,
you think she needs you.
And in her eyes you see nothing,
no sign of love behind the tears cried for no
one,
a love that should have lasted years.
You stay home, she goes out,
she says that long ago she knew someone
but now,
he's gone, she doesn't need him.
Your day breaks, your mind aches,
there will be times when all the things she
said will fill your head,
you won't forget her.
And in her eyes you see nothing,
no sign of love behind the tears cried for no
one.
A love that should have lasted years.

Golden Slumbers

Once there was a way to get back
homeward.
Once there was a way to get back home.
Sleep pretty darling do not cry,
And I will sing a lullaby.
Golden Slumbers fill your eyes,
Smiles awake you when you rise.
Sleep pretty darling do not cry,
And I will sing a lullaby.

For no one "I find it monotonous . . .
I can't make any sense out of them. I
don't think there's anything creative
or original about it. It's just loud. I
think their music won't last."–
Richard Rodgers, when asked in 1966
what he thought of the Beatles' music

Golden Slumbers "I was at my
father's house in Cheshire messing
about on the piano and I came across
the traditional tune Golden Slumbers
in a song book of Ruth's (his step-
sister). And I thought it would be nice
to write my own Golden Slumbers."
–Paul

250   <u>I'll get you</u>   "We always fight. You shout and scream and cry and all that, and then we make up— which is very nice. It's almost like treating each other as psychiatrists." — Yoko

I'll get you

Oh yeh, oh yeh.
Imagine, I'm in love with you,
it's easy 'cos I know,
I've imagined I'm in love with you,
many, many, many times before.
It's not like me to pretend,
but I'll get you in the end,
yes I will, I'll get you in the end, oh yeh,
oh yeh.
I think about you night and day,
I need you 'cos it's true.
When I think about you, I can say,
I'm never, never, never, never blue.
So I'm telling you, my friend,
that I'll get you, I'll get you in the end,
yes I will, I'll get you in the end, oh yeh,
oh yeh.
Well, there's gonna be a time,
well I'm gonna change your mind.
So you might as well resign yourself to me,
oh yeh.
Imagine, I'm in love with you,
it's easy 'cos I know,
I've imagined, I'm in love with you,
many, many, many times before.
It's not like me to pretend,
but I'll get you, I'll get you in the end,
yes I will, I'll get you in the end,
oh yeh, oh yeh.

From a window

Late yesterday night, I saw a light shine
from a window,
and as I looked again, your face came into
sight.
I couldn't walk on until you'd gone from
your window.
I had to make you mine, I knew you were
the one.
Oh, I would be so glad just to have a love
like that,
oh, I would be true and I'd live my life for
you.
So meet me tonight, just where the light
shines from a window,
and as I take your hand, say that you'll be
mine tonight.
Oh, I would be glad just to have a love like
that,
oh, I would be true and I'd live my life for
you.
So meet me tonight, just where the light
shines from a window,
and as I take your hand, say that you'll be
mine tonight.

From a window "Those who flock
round the Beatles, who scream
themselves into hysteria, whose
vacant faces flicker over the TV screen,
are the least fortunate of their
generation, the dull, the idle, the
failures . . ." – Paul Johnson writing
in the New Statesman in March 1964

Carry that weight

Boy—you're gonna carry that weight,
Carry that weight a long time.
I never give you my pillow,
I only send you my invitations,
And in the middle of the celebrations
I break down.

Carry that weight "Only Britain
hates the Beatles."—George

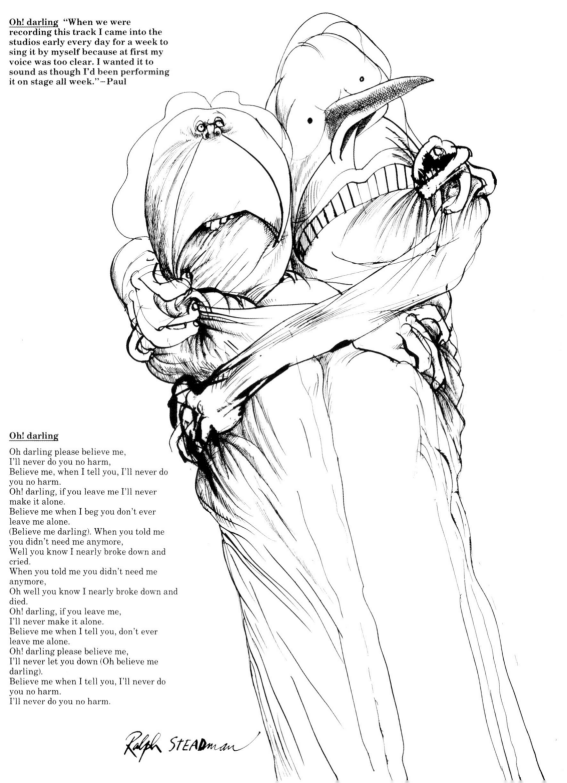

Oh! darling "When we were recording this track I came into the studios early every day for a week to sing it by myself because at first my voice was too clear. I wanted it to sound as though I'd been performing it on stage all week."–Paul

Oh! darling

Oh darling please believe me,
I'll never do you no harm,
Believe me, when I tell you, I'll never do you no harm.
Oh! darling, if you leave me I'll never make it alone.
Believe me when I beg you don't ever leave me alone.
(Believe me darling). When you told me you didn't need me anymore,
Well you know I nearly broke down and cried.
When you told me you didn't need me anymore,
Oh well you know I nearly broke down and died.
Oh! darling, if you leave me,
I'll never make it alone.
Believe me when I tell you, don't ever leave me alone.
Oh! darling please believe me,
I'll never let you down (Oh believe me darling).
Believe me when I tell you, I'll never do you no harm.
I'll never do you no harm.

Ralph STEADman

I'm happy just to dance with you "I wrote this for George to sing. I'm always reading how Paul and I used to make him invisible or keep him out, but it isn't true. I encouraged him like mad." – John

I'm happy just to dance with you

Before this dance is through,
I think I'll love you too,
I'm so happy when you dance with me.
I don't wanna kiss or hold your hand,
if it's funny, try an' understand.
There is really nothing else I'd rather do,
'cos I'm happy just to dance with you.
I don't need to hug or hold you tight,
I just wanna dance with you all night,
in this world there's nothing I would
rather do,
'cos I'm happy just to dance with you.
Just to dance with you is everything I
need,
before this dance is through,
I think I'll love you too,
I'm so happy when you dance with me.
If somebody tries to take my place,
let's pretend, we just can't see his face.
In this world there's nothing I would
rather do,
'cos I'm happy just to dance with you.
Just to dance with you is everything I
need,
before this dance is through,
I think I'll love you too,
I'm so happy, when you dance with me.
If somebody tries to take my place,
let's pretend, we just can't see his face.
In this world there's nothing I would
rather do,
I've discovered, I'm in love with you.
Oh, oh, 'cos I'm happy just to dance with
you.
Oh, oh.

Because

Because the world is round it turns me on.
Because the world is round – Ah – love is
old, love is new,
Love is all, love is you.
Because the wind is high it blows my mind.
Because the wind is high – Ah – love is old,
love is new,
Love is all, love is you.
Because the sky is blue it makes me cry.
Because the sky is blue – Ah – love is old,
love is new,
Love is all, love is you.

Because "This is about me and Yoko
in the early days. Yoko was playing
some Beethoven chords and I said play
them backwards. Its really
Moonlight Sonata backwards." – John

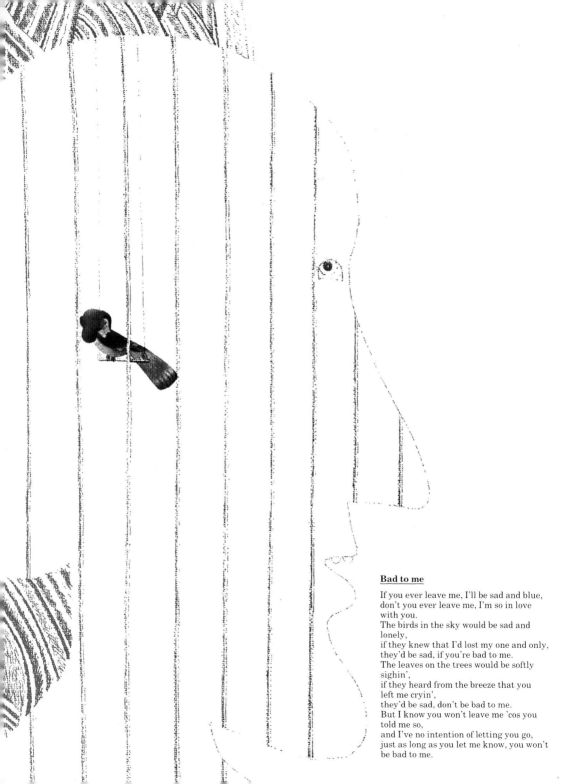

Bad to me

If you ever leave me, I'll be sad and blue,
don't you ever leave me, I'm so in love
with you.
The birds in the sky would be sad and
lonely,
if they knew that I'd lost my one and only,
they'd be sad, if you're bad to me.
The leaves on the trees would be softly
sighin',
if they heard from the breeze that you
left me cryin',
they'd be sad, don't be bad to me.
But I know you won't leave me 'cos you
told me so,
and I've no intention of letting you go,
just as long as you let me know, you won't
be bad to me.

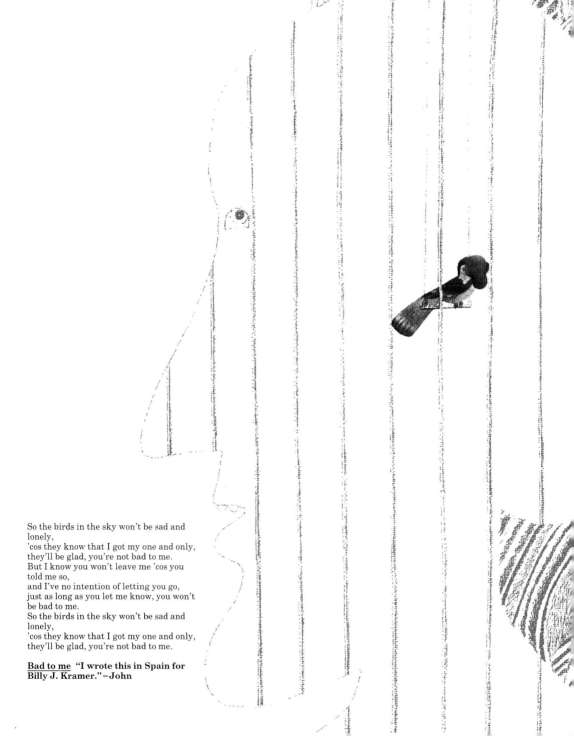

So the birds in the sky won't be sad and lonely,
'cos they know that I got my one and only,
they'll be glad, you're not bad to me.
But I know you won't leave me 'cos you told me so,
and I've no intention of letting you go,
just as long as you let me know, you won't be bad to me.
So the birds in the sky won't be sad and lonely,
'cos they know that I got my one and only,
they'll be glad, you're not bad to me.

Bad to me "I wrote this in Spain for Billy J. Kramer."−John

Ask me why

I love you,
Can't you tell me things I want to know?
And it's true that it really only goes to show
That I know that I I I I should never, never, never be blue.
Now you're mine,
My happiness still makes me cry.
And in time you'll understand the reason why
If I cry it's not because I'm sad
But you're the only one that I've ever had.
I can't believe it's happened to me.
I can't conceive of any more misery.
Ask my why
I'll say I love you and I'm always thinking of you.

Please please me

Last night I said these words to my girl
I know you never even try girl
Come on, come on, come on, come on,
Please please me oh Yeh like I please you.
You don't need me to show the way love
Why do I always have to say love
Come on, come on, come on, come on,
Please please me oh Yeh like I please you.
I don't want to sound complaining
But you know there's always rain in my heart.
I do all the pleasing with you
It's so hard to reason with you.
Oh yeh why do you make me blue.
Last night I said these words to my girl,
I know you never even try girl,
Come on, come on, come on, come on
Please please me oh Yeh like I please you–you.

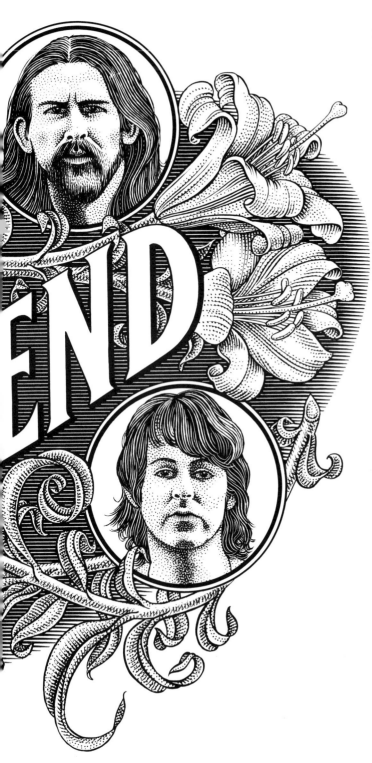

You know my name

You know my name
Look up the number
You know my name
Look up the number
You you know you know my name
You you know you know my name
Good evening and welcome to Slaggers
featuring Denis O'Bell
Come on Ringo let's hear it for Denis
Good evening
You know my name
Better look up my number
You know my name
(That's right) look up my number
You you know you know my name
You you know you know my name
You know my name
Ba ba ba ba ba ba ba ba
Look up my number
You know my name
That's right look up the number
Oh you know you know
You know my name you know you know you
know my name
Huh huh huh huh
You know my name
Ba ba ba pum
Look up the number
You know my name
Look up the number
You-a you know you know my name
Baby you-a you know you know my name
You know you know my name you know you
know my name
Go on Denis let's hear it for Denis O'Bell
You know you know you know my name you
know you know you
know my name
Purr you know my name and the number
You know my name and the number
you know you know my name
Look up me number
You know my number three
you know my number two
You know my number three
you know my number four
You know my name you know my number too
You know my name you know my number
What's up with you?
You know my name
That's right
Yeah

The end

Oh yeah alright, are you gonna be in my
dreams tonight.
And in the end the love you take is equal
to the love you make.
Ah—

**The end "I didn't leave the Beatles.
The Beatles have left the Beatles—but
no one wants to be the one to say the
party's over." – Paul**

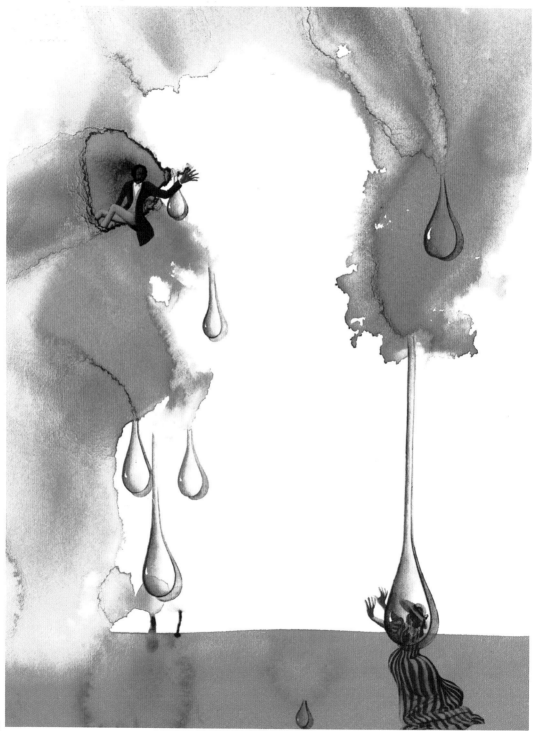

I'll follow the sun

One day you'll look to see I've gone,
for tomorrow may rain so I'll follow the
sun.
Some day you'll know I was the one,
but tomorrow may rain so I'll follow the
sun.
And now the time has come and so my
love I must go,
and though I lose a friend in the end you
will know, oh.
One day you'll find that I have gone,
but tomorrow may rain so I'll follow the
sun
And now the time has come and so my love
I must go,
and though I lose a friend in the end you
will know oh.
One day you'll find that I have gone,
but tomorrow may rain so I'll follow the
sun.

**I'll follow the sun "Our life on the
farm in Scotland is the real life. It's
very rough up there but it's the life
I've always dreamed about. I love
nature. When I was a kid we used to
go on nature rambles with the school
and I used to love it when the master
told us all about the different
birds."–Paul**

Goodbye

Please don't wake me until late tomorrow
comes,
And I will not be late.
Late today when it becomes tomorrow,
I will leave to go away.
Goodbye, goodbye, goodbye, goodbye my
love goodbye.
Songs that lingered on my lips excite me
now
And linger on my mind.
Leave your flowers at my door
I'll leave then for the one who waits
behind.
Far away my lover sings a lonely song
And calls me to his side.
When the song of lonely love
Invites me on I must go to his side.
Goodbye, goodbye, goodbye, goodbye my
love goodbye.

**Goodbye "I don't intend to be a
performing flea anymore. I was the
dreamweaver, but although I'll be
around I don't intend to be running at
20,000 miles an hour trying to prove
myself. I don't want to die at 40."
–John**

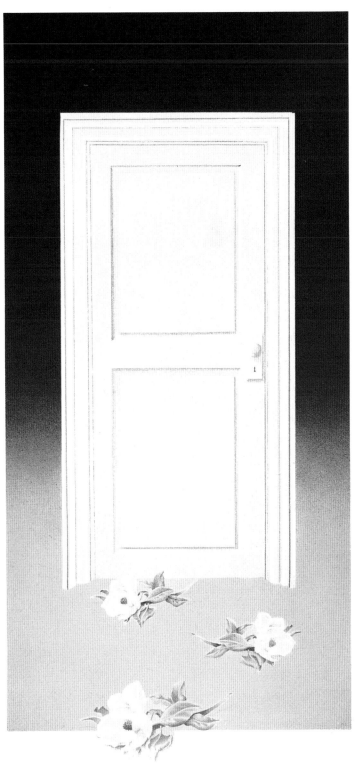

INDEX

Acknowledgements

This book could not have been compiled without a great deal of help. Because of space, it is not possible to mention everyone by name, but we should like to express our thanks to all the people who took part in its production, particularly Art Kane, who started the ball rolling, and the contributors who produced pictures for little reward. We are also indebted to the fans whose response to our ads was astonishing: Ken White, Thelma Cowen, Alan Birch, Allan Jones, Frances Platt, G. Dean, Molly Booth, David Wright, Anita Johnson, Carole Smith, Tony Rushton, Doreen Hyde, Joan Langford, Richard Phillips, Shennel Rothman, Terry Hynes, Hilary Petch, Dennis McKeown, Irene Hanson, B. Cawson, L. Baker, Martin Lawson, Stephen McGee, Joanne Thomson, F. Ashcroft, Christine and Pauline Westley, S. McCarthy, Pat Laythorpe, Alan Crawley, Stewart Emmott, S. Hurst, V. McCartney, C. Hanne, P. Stennet, Jan Moller, B. Cohen, Allan Le Carpentier, K. Voels, Kevin Day, Mike Davies, Alan Platt and many others whom we have forgotten. Special assistance in the design of the book was provided by David Hillman and Gilvrie Misstear, and Bob Smithers, James Marsh and Harry Willock sweated through many sleepless nights building models and spraying colours. We should also like to thank Ray Connolly, who prepared the captions, and to David Wild, Barbara Swiderska and Juliet Robson for their decorations. We would like to thank Heinemann for giving us their kind permission to publish extracts from THE BEATLES: the authorised biography by Hunter Davies. The illustration of Eduardo Paolozzi is reproduced by kind permission of the Petersburg Press.

Author Biography

Alan Aldridge left school when he was 15, then drifted through a multiplicity of jobs. He was an insurance clerk, a barrow boy and an actor in repertory. When he was 20 he started to draw. That was in 1968. Today he is one of the great original forces at work in the world of creative graphics. His style is distinctive and immediate, fantasy with a hard edge. His design and use of colour has inspired many imitators, none of whom has yet matched his own idiosyncratic vision. He has won many design awards, including a silver medal from the Designers and Art Directors Association and The Scotsman International Design Award twice, and his work is a familiar feature of Britain's magazines, advertisement billboards and record covers.